CONTENTS

Introduction

References

ABOUT THE AUTHOR

Ernest Theodossin was born and educated to first degree level (University of Michigan) in the United States. He came to Britain as a postgraduate student (University of London), began a teaching career in English (schools, a technical college, a college of education) and became a naturalised British subject. In the mid-seventies he retrained (University of London Institute of Education) in educational administration and management and taught (university, institute of higher education) in this field before joining the Further Education Staff College as a staff tutor. Both his doctorate and much of his subsequent research have been in the management of planned change, in which area he has previously published **Management restructuring in an FE college** (FESC 1984). He is currently Deputy Director of the Responsive College Programme, funded by the MSC, led by the staff college, and intended to promote the development of a marketing approach to work-related NAFE in colleges of further education.

INTRODUCTION

The project on which this book is based began to take shape in January 1985. Prior to becoming Director of the Further Education Staff College (FESC) in December of the previous year, Geoffrey Melling started to explore with the Manpower Services Commission (MSC) a possible action programme on 'The Responsive College'. Such a programme would involve FESC staff leading field workers in a group of regional projects designed to promote enhanced responsiveness of colleges of further education (CFEs) to the training needs of industry and commerce. The focus would be on non-advanced further education (NAFE), and the intention was to identify/-develop good practice in programme colleges, with a view to promoting dissemination and take-up across the further education (FE) system.

Melling and Dr Derek Birch, FESC's Deputy Director in charge of the staff college's research/consultancy activities, asked me to carry out a 'ground clearing exercise' as a preliminary exploration for the larger programme. The idea was to spend something like four months in devising a conceptual framework for the action programme and in seeking possible answers to fundamental questions: What is a responsive college? Which are the responsive colleges? What distinguishes such institutions from the non-responsive variety?

The prototype which Melling had in mind was **In search of excellence: lessons from America's best-run companies** by Thomas J. Peters and Robert H. Waterman, Jr. (1982). Peters/Waterman had set out to draw up

> . . . a list of companies considered to be innovative and excellent by an informed group of observers of the business scene - businessmen, consultants, members of the business press, and business academics.

and from their analysis of these organisations had identified

> . . . eight attributes that emerged to characterise most nearly the distinction of the excellent, innovative companies . . .

Why not undertake a similar odyssey in work-related NAFE and seek to identify distinguishing characteristics among 'excellent, innovative' colleges? By comparison my efforts would have to be obviously and strikingly modest: even with MSC funding, I lacked anything like comparable resources. Peters/Waterman had 'put together a team' and conducted 'a full-blown project on the subject of excellence'. Their colleagues had analysed 'press coverage and annual reports for the last twenty-five years' for each of their specimen companies. I was to work with a research assistant, Charlie Mason, and to have seventeen weeks to conceive, carry out and write up the FESC/MSC project. On the other hand, Peters/Waterman were looking at the **whole** of the United States business world, and my field of enquiry was in comparison almost miniscule: in England and Wales[1], there are approximately 550 colleges and polytechnics employing 'some 90,000 lecturers' and with a student population 'equivalent to 900,000 full-time students', the whole representing gross expenditure of 'over £2 billion a year' (Audit Commission, 1985). Peters/Waterman's sample had included 'few firms' with 'annual sales of less than $1 billion'. Given that all things are relative, might I not attempt/achieve a production at least 'in the school of' the masters?

Peters/Waterman ceased to be a dominating influence at a very early stage of the project. Drawing upon the views of their 'informed group of observers', they had produced a list of 62 companies and then decided that

> ... no matter what prestige these companies had in the eyes of the rest of the business world, the companies were not truly excellent unless their financial performance supported their halo of esteem.

and gone on to reduce their original 62 companies to 43 by imposing 'six measures of long-term superiority': compound asset/equity growth from 1961 through 1980; average ratio of market value to book value; average return on total capital, 1961 through 1980; average returns on equity sales, 1961 through 1980. In other words, they were able to define, identify and measure excellence in American business; I achieved nothing comparable with responsiveness in British NAFE. They had quantifiable data; I had opinions and intuitive evaluation. Theirs was the hard world of income, expenditure and profit, sales figures, market value; mine was the soft world of debate and assertion, claim and counterclaim.

The original plan, drawn up with Derek Birch and Charlie Mason, encompassed a three-phased enquiry: explore the literature on college responsiveness; identify and interview 'an informed group of observers' of the NAFE scene with a view to locating excellent/responsive colleges; interview in such colleges to discern what 'characterises most nearly the distinction' of the excellent/responsive college. I found very little in the literature which dealt **explicitly** with college responsiveness, apart from a growing interest in 'market research', an epithet rapidly acquiring almost talismanic powers. Of course, there is a vast body of material dealing with client-organisation relations, much of it American and drawn from non-education settings, but, given the limitations of both time and space, I have resisted the temptation to extrapolate and adapt. Similarly with the popular educational press which has in recent months produced much where, by implication and between the lines, we may uncover inferences/-assumptions about college responsiveness. Here, too, I have favoured restraint, and generally (if not always) avoided the practice of finding 'tongues in trees, books in the running brooks, sermons in stones': the list of

---

1. The Scottish scene is noted later.

references is deliberately short[2]. Conversely, I have quoted fairly frequently from that still small (but growing) body of work which deals **directly** with current issues in college/client relationships.

In terms of the second and third phases of our intended plan, the 'informed group of observers' offered scores of colleges perceived as wholly or partly responsive and scores of criteria by which to measure college responsiveness, but here was little that could be described as consensual. The 'halo of esteem' seemed to be worn by many from time to time, and seldom for the same reason(s). It was ultimately impossible to draw up an authoritative list of excellent/responsive colleges. The third phase of the enquiry never materialised. What follows is therefore fundamentally centred on evidence provided (and, sometimes, more interestingly, omitted) by our respondents, and, as such, can be said to reflect a wide spectrum of current attitudes, and to focus attention on the inherent difficulties of defining, identifying and promoting responsiveness.

At least part of the explanation must lie in the sheer novelty of responsiveness as an important goal in education/training in a system which has traditionally been provider- rather than client-centred. To my eyes at least, many respondents betrayed by their lengthy and thoughtful pauses before answering questions that they were examining issues to which they had given limited previous thought. Such a conclusion is not intended as a criticism, but rather as a recognition that responsiveness has only very recently become a topic of public debate. At the same time, it would be fair to acknowledge that some might wish to suggest that the topic is anything but new, that FE has been concerned with responsiveness for generations, and that we have simply happened upon another instance of new language (jargon) being used to dress up old ideas. There is some truth in the assertion. One can often find an overlap between old concerns and new preoccupations. However, **some** is not all. In the sixties, one strand of argument in the comprehensivisation debate was based on the claim that public schools had been comprehensive for generations since their pupils were drawn from rich and poor backgrounds and were both more and less academically able, to which a frequent response was, 'Yes, but . . .' And so with responsiveness.

The stimulus for the current debate can be very precisely identified: the Government White Paper **Training for jobs** (DE/DES, 1984) in which we are told that

> The public sector needs a greater incentive to relate the courses it provides more closely to the needs of the customer and in the most cost effective way[3].

2. I have also not drawn upon a fairly extensive body (some six inches thick) of material made available by respondents and others, allegedly dealing with responsiveness but (with few exceptions) touching upon the subject only tangentially.
3. The concern with cost effectiveness has been taken up by the Adult Commission (1985).

and the report **Competence and competition** (NEDC/MSC, 1984) which urges colleges to

> ... go to their potential customers with the offer of providing for their needs and wishes at times and in ways which suit the individual. They should 'market' rather than 'sell', and make customers welcome on their own terms rather than pressing them into college convenience. They should persuade people to look on the education service as an ally, counsellor and friend.

Understandably, much resentment has been aroused among professionals whose work is either centred in, or primarily related to, the activities of colleges. Both documents make unsubstantiated allegations which are subsequently used as a basis for exhortation. FE's response has encompassed hurt, resentment, anger and unsubstantiated counter-assertions. The issue is either a pretext (a manufactured crisis) for central government takeover and the destruction of local government autonomy; or, from the other side, such a takeover is necessitated by the current inadequacy of local provision. **Responsibility and responsiveness** (Kedney/Parkes, 1984) opens with a challenging preface:

> ... The White Paper, **Training for jobs** (1984), contained neither evidence nor argument to justify the Government's belief that the Manpower Services Commission can make vocational education more responsive to the training needs of industry and commerce. On the other hand, the record shows that the colleges have demonstrated over the years their capacity to perceive local needs for training and education and their flexibility in satisfying them. Whatever deficiencies exist in our provision for vocational education, the local education authorities and their colleges are the least culpable of all the responsible parties.

followed by eight case studies in which interested parties asserted their responsiveness. The truth, however, is that there is no 'record' on which either side can rely, beyond a quantity of frequently conflicting impressions. There is no data because there is no agreement about what data might be useful, or, indeed, whether any data might be appropriate. Peters/Waterman may have been able to substantiate the judgements of their 'informed group of observers' by reference to 'financial performance': in education/training, we have nothing comparable.

The search for excellence led me into uncharted waters in which I glimpsed land only occasionally and never disembarked, although the travel itself was not without absorbing interests and stimulating discoveries. The following pages offer a log of that voyage.

As indicated above, I was fortunate in having the assistance of Charlie Mason in all of the work prior to the writing up of the report. Without his

4

highly professional support it would not have been possible to complete the project in the time available. The analysis and the text are entirely my own so that I alone must be held accountable for what follows. At the completion of the first draft Charlie provided me with extremely helpful critical notes, as did Geoff Melling, Derek Birch and David Parkes, all of which I drew upon for emendations. I am grateful for the thoughtful assistance of these colleagues, although I would wish to bear responsibility for any faults or failures.

It remains to be recorded that the MSC funded the project totally, while in no way seeking to constrain or direct the activity. I wish to express my gratitude for the support and the freedom.

Chapter 1

THE ENQUIRY

In seeking to identify a group of respondents equivalent to Peters-/Waterman's 'informed group of observers', individuals with a broad and detailed knowledge of NAFE, we set ourselves the following guidelines.

1. **Focus.** While we recognised that FE is expected to serve the needs of a wide range of client groups, our project was primarily concerned with exploring the claim advanced in **Training for jobs** (DE/DES, 1984) and **Competence and competition** (NEDO/MSC, 1984): that FE was failing adequately to meet the needs of industry and commerce. In practice this meant that we should seek to draw upon the experience of those who had 'across the boundary' knowledge of the industry/college relationship[1].

2. **Breadth.** In order to facilitate comparison, it was important that we seek out individuals likely to have present dealings with several colleges rather than a single institution. This effectively excluded both students and most college staff. The principals we selected were identified as having 'system roles', as occupying themselves at least a part of the time in multi-college associations, e.g. the Association of Principals of Colleges (APC), the National Association of Teachers in Further and Higher Education (NATFHE).

3. **Depth.** Wherever possible, we should interview people who had operated across the college/industry boundary for some time, people with more than a passing acquaintance with the system.

4. **Range.** The respondent groups whom we questioned ought to include representation from industry/commerce and trades unions, the Department of Education and Science (DES), the Further Education Unit (FEU), validating bodies and local authorities (LAs). Additionally, we decided to seek out the perceptions of Members of Parliament (MPs), so as to take account of the views of those involved (or likely to be) in policy promotion at central level; of private individuals working as educational consultants and with a foot in both camps; and of voluntary organisation representatives, not necessarily directly concerned with the industry/college relationship, but likely to represent the interests of other client groups potentially in conflict over college priorities in a period of limited resources.

We drew upon our own and our colleagues' 'networks' to identify potential respondents. We accepted the advice of individual respondents. We asked organisations to nominate interviewees.

---

1. Some of the other client groups are considered in later chapters.

Between 8 May and 2 August 1985, we interviewed 54 individuals, on five occasions with pairs of respondents and on the remaining 44 in one-to-one situations. The shortest interview was approximately a half hour and the longest nearly three hours, with most occupying between one and two hours. The majority of respondents were generous with their time and answered our questions thoughtfully. Our interview schedule is included in Appendix A. Our intention was to allow respondents to do most of the talking rather than to enter into debate. Some of the questions were deliberately repetitive to allow individuals to confront the same issues at different points in the interview, and not all of the questions were necessarily appropriate for all respondents, for which reason upon occasion respondents stated their inability to reply to particular questions. At the end of the interview we encouraged our interviewees to make additional points or raise issues they considered might have been omitted, and it was at this stage that much interesting material was offered.

The immediate purpose of the interview schedule was to elicit responses to eight basic questions, viz.

1. What is a responsive college?

2. To whom is a responsive college responding?

3. How does the college deal with conflict among competing client demands?

4. What criteria can be used to identify/measure college responsiveness?

5. Which colleges are currently perceived as responsive?

6. What distinguishes such colleges from the non-responsive kind?

7. What obstacles currently exist to responsiveness?

8. What can be/has been done to make colleges more responsive?

In both the research instrument and the actual interviewing, these questions were sometimes put more obliquely and upon occasion, as already indicated, more than once, partly for corroboration, partly to allow some issues to be examined both negatively and positively (e.g. responsiveness and non-responsiveness), and partly to let individuals explore their own feelings about issues they had not necessarily thought through carefully, a fact to which some made explicit reference. The material in the following chapters has been organised roughly along the lines of the above questions.

As has already been explained, our sample was deliberately biased and was concentrated upon the expectations of what might be described as a single market segment, industry/commerce. Our industrial respondents included representatives of the Confederation of British Industry (CBI), manufacturing and service industries, chambers of commerce, both public and private sectors; our union sample included the Trades Union Congress (TUC) and the National Association of Teachers in Further and Higher Education (NATFHE). We spoke with principals and (deviating from our original intention) several heads of department because they allowed us to obtain a college perspective of a particular local industry/college relationship. We sought out Her Majesty's Inspectorate (HMI) and civil servants (in the DES and MSC), local authority officers and advisers, validating body national and regional staff, additionally searching for perspectives on a number of national industry/college initiatives: Professional, Industrial and Commercial Updating (PICKUP), College Employer Links Project (CELP) and Local Collaborative Projects (LCPs). We interviewed representatives from the FEU, voluntary organisations and the major Parliamentary parties (expect for the Liberals whose representative proved elusive). We also talked with educational consultants.

In looking over our list of respondents, one might at first consider it useful to organise them into 'interest groups' and to attempt to present a group perspective, what MSC 'thinks' or what the DES 'believes'. This proved inappropriate for the following reasons:

1. Our sub-group samples were too small to be representative. Even with our largest interest group sample, representatives of industry/commerce, we had just over a dozen, hardly large enough for a proper survey.[2]

2. The overwhelming majority of our respondents were in the second half of their professional careers and many of them did not fit exclusively into a single group: several of our educational consultants had worked in colleges; one MSC respondent was an ex-principal, another an ex-LEA officer; a DES civil servant had started as a college lecturer, etc. Often our respondents therefore spoke from a wealth of background experience from under a variety of proverbial 'hats'.

3. Nothing clearly representative of an identifiable interest group view emerged. Respondents frequently shared perceptions, but generally 'across' formally definable interest groups. For example, criticism of industry's role in the industry/college relationship might be expected to emerge from those working on the college side of the boundary: it did. However, some of the sharpest criticism of industry came from industrial, chamber of commerce, and MSC respondents. Large organisations invariably employ staff with a wide spectrum of attitudes and perceptions.

For the above reasons, I decided to treat our respondents either as individuals or as proportional groups of the whole sample, i.e. 'nearly a third of our respondents . . .' In order to enable me to quote freely from the interview transcripts, I have omitted names but identified their

2. Much research (including Peters/Waterman) is vague about data interview sources and numbers.

organisations, frequently endowing individuals with the sobriquets 'Officer' or 'Official': hence MSC Officer or DES Official. I have preserved a similar kind of anonymity with particular employers and colleges. There are obvious losses, but I hope greater insights into real attitudes and an absence of that kind of bland, balanced and neutral statement to which so many educationists resort in public utterance. Paradoxically (or perhaps not) our most cautious respondents proved to be two of our sample of principals whose colleges, we were assured, were not only totally responsive to **all** local (and even international) needs, but unsullied by a knowledge of conflict. Such innocence was rare.

As has already been indicated, our literature search produced limited results. Frequently there was nothing explicit about responsiveness, but implicit assumptions relating to the industry/college relationship, for which reason I have occasionally noted (and acknowledged as such) the unintended. At the same time, there is a growing body of writing addressed to what the Audit Commission (1985) calls 'strengthening the marketing of further education'. I have drawn upon this fairly extensively. From both the interview and literature quotations it is intended that the whole range of current perceptions of the relationship between industry and further education should be made explicit. Whether such perceptions are accurate either wholly or partly is another matter, and one to which I turn in the final chapters. However, just or otherwise, informed or prejudiced, such attitudes form part of the context in which college and local authority managers are expected to provide a public sector service.

Chapter 2

THE MISSIONARY AND THE MARKETEER: WHAT ARE COLLEGES FOR?

We began, unexceptionably, by trying to ascertain what our respondents saw as the purpose of CFEs: starting by attempting to clarify assumptions and agree definitions offers the possibility of establishing a secure foundation. In further education, however, precise definitions are notoriously difficult to attain, and it is likely that in a service provision which overlaps with both schools and higher education, and which offers both award- and non-award-bearing courses[1] for work and play, agreed definitions might be neither likely nor useful. NATFHE, for example, in its submission to the Joint MSC/LAA Working Group on Work Related NAFE (1985), makes great play of

> ... the lack of an adequate definition for 'work related NAFE' ... It would seem reasonable to start from the premise that virtually all non-advanced further education is work-related. This would include the full range of GCE O and A level subjects to a greater or lesser extent, in that they provide access to vocational or professional qualification courses.

Indeed, in a society in which so little work requires legal licensing by formal qualifications, almost any kind of experience, in and out of CFEs, can serve as a prelude to employment.

The difficulties are compounded by an underlying dichotomy in the world of education and training. In Britain, education has been historically associated with the Church: the monastic tradition, foundation/voluntary schools and colleges, and involvement with teacher training, overseas mission work in the days of empire, the Protestant work ethic, Victorian values. The law still requires those undergoing compulsory education to begin their day's learning with an act of corporate worship. Of course, with the passage of time and the decline of church attendance, the specifically Christian nature of the provision and of the institutions embodying it has often faded. Nonetheless, the tradition and the impulse survive. Much of what goes on in our classrooms is seen by at least some teachers as part of a proselytizing process: converting, changing attitudes, saving, revealing new possibilities, bringing hope to the unfortunate, opportunities to the lost. For

1. Forty per cent of NAFE enrolments are for courses which do not lead to specific qualifications. (MSC/LAA, 1985)

11

many, the traditional passion for conversion, the *vocational* dimension of the teaching role, has been metamorphosed into a commitment to social engineering, and the fervour of that commitment is what sustains them in an otherwise routine and repetitive job.

We have seen since the 1944 Education Act a broad professional commitment to education as a social transformation process. In the 1960s and the 1970s we were exhorted to comprehensivise, to banish organisational differentiation and distinction, to teach in mixed-ability groups, and in so doing to modify society painlessly, bringing educational success to those previously rejected, extending the take-up of higher and further education, blurring social class divisions. In the 1980s we are being urged to provide for socially disadvantaged groups: women, ethnic minorities, the disabled, the unemployed. By encouraging the insecure, we can promote and stimulate the development of personal confidence. By placing blacks and women in high-status institutional roles, we can erode stereotypes and raise aspirations. There is about the advocacy of such activities something of the flavour of a crusade, and about adherents to such causes the aura of *the missionary*. Their commitment is to doing good to others, helping, bringing comfort and compassion. It is an essentially paternalistic (or maternalistic) approach, a conviction that the missionary is right and the unconverted unfortunate. One might argue that the missionary approach is deeply embedded within the profession, perhaps more fully in schools and higher education than in CFEs, but everywhere evident to some extent. The missionary is interested not in partial or immediate achievement, but in developing the whole person for a whole lifetime. The missionary is concerned with education rather than training. Clearly it is impossible to determine the extent to which the missionary role is espoused by the teaching profession, or even whether among adherents the commitment is constant. One may suspect that for some, a missionary dimension emerges from time to time as convenient, and that public utterance is not always sustained in private action. On the other hand, the missionary zeal often seems to lie unexpectedly just below the surface. For example, the DES/HMI **Teacher training and preparation for working life** (1982) concludes, inevitably, that

> It is important that industrial and commercial relevance of the school curriculum should be an integral part of the institution's planning for the initial training course as a whole ...

but *en passant* admits that

> Preparing pupils for adult working life is not the only task of teachers, nor is a knowledge of industry and commerce the only skill a teacher needs to be effective in this field. The most important preparation is still a sound basic education, coupled with an ability to work with others ...

The difficulties here are twofold. Firstly, there is no real professional consensus about what constitutes 'a sound basic education' or which of any agreed components is more/less important than any other: the missionaries are multi-denominational. Secondly, educating the whole person for a whole lifetime is in essence an act of faith in that, in a practical sense, no one can either prove or disprove success/failure. For most learners, the teacher is neither going to know the whole person nor be around for the whole of his lifetime, for which reasons such lofty aspirations are likely to be viewed as sophistry by more practical individuals. One of our respondents, a CBI spokesperson, was particularly scathing about the principal

> . . . who is anti-industry and talks about the 'whole person' and 'bull' of that kind.

The other adversary in our education/training dichotomy, *the marketeer* ('one who sells in a market': OED), is both more and less evident in CFEs, or is at least perceived to be so by different observers. Whatever the precise definition of 'work-related NAFE', colleges have traditionally been associated with preparing people for work roles in industry/commerce and with upgrading the skills of those already in such roles. Colleges have for long been turning out secretaries, engineers, office workers, hairdressers, caterers, etc. Many college staff came into teaching from an industrial/commercial background, and CFE teachers have uniquely for long had clearly defined conditions of service, currently embodied in the NATFHE Silver Book. The organisation culture of a college, in its emphasis on the quantitative assessment of teacher effort and its elaborate system of remission and constraints in managerial deployment of teachers, remains strikingly different from what we may encounter in schools or universities.[2] Of all educational establishments, CFEs are undoubtedly closest in their *modus operandi* to what one finds in industry/commerce. The point in dispute is whether they are close enough.

From the industrial/commercial point of view, the major failings of CFEs may be summarised as:

1. **Inflexibility.** Colleges are perceived as essentially provider- rather than client-centred, concerned to sell their existing courses at times and in ways which are convenient to college staff: eager only to locate 'horses for courses', i.e. to fit potential students to the demands of existing courses. There is a disinclination to offer customised provision. Colleges have difficulty in starting any course except in September and are closed for 14 weeks of the year.

2. **Slowness.** When they are prepared to change, colleges seem to require extraordinary periods of notice: with their elaborate committee structures and bureaucratic procedures, and their commitment to a democratic-

---

2. Cf. current attempts to get schoolteachers to agree conditions of service and Government determination to limit university tenure.

/consensual style ('everyone getting in on the act'), colleges are cumbersome and incapable of moving rapidly in response to anything.

3. **Out of touch and out of date.** Some college staff are hostile to industry/commerce[3] and do not seem to appreciate that Britain is a manufacturing/trading nation whose prosperity depends on its ability to create wealth. Those teachers who are not aggressively unsympathetic to industry/commerce have generally had their last period of industrial experience so long ago that they are now preparing students for a work world which no longer exists.

4. **Expensive.** CFEs are over-resourced and inefficient, for which reason their courses are over-priced.

5. **Accountability.** Because employers subsidise colleges heavily through the rates system, colleges owe it to their providers to reorganise themselves to become more responsive to industrial/commercial needs.

In turn, from a CFE perspective, employers may be criticised for the following:

1. **Inarticulateness.** Through their representation on a whole range of advisory committees, and through provision for involvement in validating body course development, employers have opportunities for making their needs known. Unfortunately, employers either do not know what they want/need, or are incapable of communicating the information clearly.

2. **Conflicting/competing demands.** There are as many employer 'needs' as there are employers. Even when the CBI makes its wants known, it does not necessarily speak for the thousands of small employers. Often an individual college has many hundreds of individual employers whose needs it is attempting to serve, and the needs of one are not necessarily congruent with the needs of others.

3. **Lack of resources.** In recent years colleges have had to bear increasing cuts in resources. Offering customised provision is, unfortunately, expensive. So, too, are visiting employers to discuss provision needs, mounting courses for small groups, sending staff back into industry, extending opening hours/days.

4. **Selfishness.** Employers often talk as if **their** needs were the only needs with which the college need concern itself. In fact, colleges exist to serve the needs of the whole community, not merely those of employers. Often the needs of other client groups are not compatible with those of industry/commerce. In many parts of the country, students leave college not for work but for unemployment. The college cannot morally justify

3. 'The use of the term 'vocational' pejoratively by educationalists has a long history and when applied to a body of work can be an effective blocking mechanism to real thought about its actual character'. (Flower, 1981)

serving one client group at the expense of the others.

5. **Short-term goals.** Employers are concerned with immediate profitability. They are inclined to regard employees as expendable and/or interchangeable. The college has a responsibility to prepare students for the longer term and not merely to develop skills which can be exploited by employers to meet immediate needs.

6. **Values.** All of human activity cannot be judged in terms of profitability. The college - and the education system as a whole - has a moral responsibility to look after the needs of disadvantaged individuals/groups: there are social, as well as industrial/commercial, needs to be considered. Man shall not live by bread alone.

The above is, of course, a caricature. There are undoubtedly hundreds, and perhaps thousands, of exceptions. **Responsibility and responsiveness** (Kedney/Parkes, 1985), to which I have referred previously, offers eight exceptions in the form of case studies and notes they

> . . . could, perhaps with a little licence, be reflecting the output and a great deal of the flexibility of a single responsive further education college.

The problem is that we have no way of knowing to what extent such caricatures are valid/invalid. They certainly occur over and over again in the interview evidence we have collected, and as such they will be discussed in subsequent chapters. What is, however, central to our concern here is that such caricatures are founded on sets of partially conflicting first principles. The industrial/commercial caricature of colleges is consistently that of the marketeer: in the market-place we all want to buy the services we require at the lowest price compatible with an acceptable quality level, and when and as convenient to our needs. On the other hand, the college caricature of industry/commerce draws upon responses derived from both the marketeer (lack of resources, cuts) and the missionary (responsibility and morality) perspectives.

The division is deeply embedded in the teaching profession and represents at worst a kind of schizophrenia, at best a two-sided coin which can be turned as appropriate, depending on what we wish to defend. The resulting uncertainty crops up, as we shall see, over and over in the reflections of our respondents, but it occurs, too, in the literature:

> Colleges should . . . 'market' rather than 'sell' . . . (NEDC/MSC, 1984).

> All colleges have entered this new world of the market, though they insist it is secondary to their educational objectives. (Kedney/Parkes, 1985).

> While the term 'marketing' is a relatively new one to NAFE, the

system has been continuously and energetically engaged in marketing for many years. (NATFHE, 1985).

. . . there is disturbing evidence from auditors' reports that in many instances colleges are not marketing their facilities well. (Audit Commission, 1985).

The development of FE has been principally concerned with its supporting role to commerce and industry - the imparting of knowledge and skills associated solely or chiefly with improved performance in jobs. (DES, 1983)

Missionary or marketeer, education or training, focused on individual or on workplace needs: we can find support for each and both views. Among our respondents, there were few who wished to advance themselves purely as missionaries. Perhaps the current allegation of college failure to meet employer needs has made individuals defensive. Possibly we as researchers were perceived as advocating a marketeer approach. Whatever the reason, only a Labour MP, furthest from the college scene, was unwaveringly proselytizing:

The fundamental aim should be to enlarge life opportunities, including judgements about how people can perform in the local economy. What the employer says is only part of the provision, so there is another dimension, not just the labour market.

A LA Training Officer saw education, rather than training, as the means of making the worker more effective in his job:

I tend to think they are there to prepare students for work, so they are not naive when they come to us. BTEC doesn't equip people to work, but it prepares them . . . We send staff to the CFE to broaden their outlook and knowledge. It offers them a wider setting and awareness, but they are not at the CFE to get skills. They are there to get an education, e.g. oral presentation . . .

Several other respondents indicated support for both marketeer and missionary, with a predeliction for the latter:

The CFE should be delivering relevant comprehensive prog-rammes, formal and non-formal, relevant to the needs of individuals and employers and the community, presupposing that one can identify individual needs. It should also include adult life training (effectiveness and efficiency) and understanding the world in order to function as part of the wider community. (Deputy Education Officer)

CFEs have two functions: 1) to be responsive and to provide

training for industry and commerce, so this function is dictated by industry, and 2) CFEs are in the business to offer a general education for life. CFEs shouldn't just be serving industry. It is difficult to state priorities, but, if you threaten to shoot me if I don't, I would have to say that the priority is offering a general education for life. If you can't afford both this and training for industry and commerce, then the 'purity of life argument' comes first. (Director of Education)

A larger group of individuals were unreservedly committed to a marketeer approach:

... responding to industrial needs in a vocational sense to get to jobs, to make people employable. We are putting sixteen-year-olds through a system that used to end in a job, but not any more. But I don't subscribe to education for leisure. Although some people in the college do, I can't accept it. (Head of Department)

The college is there to serve the needs of local business and the industrial community. It's an ongoing and continuing activity. The learning should be increasingly modular, tailor-made, learner-centred as opposed to teacher-centred. There should be open learning, flexibility, rapid response. (CBI Officer)

I see colleges providing off-the-job training and education ... integrated training. If they don't do it, we'll have to set up training centres ... It's not only a matter of meeting needs, but levels of ability and different learning rates. Everybody starting 6 September and doing the same lessons doesn't make too much sense. (ITB Officer)

The college is a business. (Principal)

Yet the overwhelming majority of our respondents sought in their definitions of college purpose to encompass the goals of both missionary and marketeer, differing only in the role which they put first:

CFEs exist to assist late developers, provide post-school education (formal qualifications), and provide vocational training (this is their weakest area). (Industrial Trainer)

The college has two responsibilities: 1) to the locality, to find out local requirements of kids and adults from industry in order to make sure industry and commerce have the trained and motivated people they need . . . 2) nationally to listen to Government and to take it into account if there is a conflict . . . Colleges are not responsible for everything. Effort has to be aimed at wealth creation and colleges should support local industry and commerce. Closely following this responsibility is that to the local unemployed. (Industrial Trainer)

CFEs have an educational role as represented in the 1944 Act and the function of responding to the training needs of industry. This is becoming more apparent and some colleges are switched on, but the quality varies between colleges. (ITB Officer)

Colleges should be meeting the needs of industry/commerce and individuals (not necessarily in that order) . . . Politicians sometimes think skills centres and colleges should be similar. I myself would go to a private trainer to learn keyboard skills, but I would want my secretary to go to a college or a secretarial college to gain something more. (MSC Officer)

A college has a dual function: 1) to service the individual, 2) within a context provided by the community and the economic community. My own view is that there has to be a careful balance between them. The priority has to be the students, but not absolutely. (Educational Consultant)

Many CFEs were born out of industry, so historically they were a support service to the community. I'd like to see them doing more for adults and see them changing. They have become 'bogged down'. (Chamber of Commerce Officer)

The function of colleges is 1) to offer education opportunity beyond schools (further is the operative word), and 2) to try and have courses linked into local industry and commerce, e.g. in Norfolk agriculture courses should be available. (Conservative MP)

The education/training, missionary/marketeer functions both reflect and perpetuate a duality of purpose in which potentially conflicting ends are uneasily yoked together, as in the familiar epithet, 'Vocational Education and Training' (VET). Spoken rapidly enough, the phrase half hints at some kind of integration. Analysing the components individually exposes the underlying tension: ultimately, if only implicitly, one must be either a missionary or a marketeer when one cannot be both.[4] One solution to this dilemma seized upon by another group of respondents was to take a broader, holistic view: the college is there to do everything.

The college exists to serve community needs. (Principal)

4. Cracknell (1983) argues against the notion that there is a 'fundamental contradiction between preparing young people for making a living in society and at the same time emphasising the development of their intellect' and suggests that 'resolving apparent and actual conflict is central to teaching strategies, curriculum planning and education management'. There is, of course, a difference between ideal-state theorising and the pressures/constraints of the real world.

Colleges can have both NAFE and AFE ... AFE responds to national provision. NAFE is defined in the local community for individuals, bearing in mind local labour markets. It also includes non-work related activity, and there is no definition of that. (NATFHE Officer)

... to respond to the needs of the population as determined by the employers and the population together. (Deputy Staff Manager, Nationalised Industry)

The function of CFEs is to meet the expressed needs of the people in its catchment area which, within its resources, it can train and educate. My personal view is that colleges should meet those needs which are most severe in extent and depth. Which needs is a question which the LEA, not the college, should decide. (Voluntary Organisation Researcher)

... responding to the needs of the community, including employers. (FEU Officer)

The function of the CFE is to provide topping up after school to offer a second chance to under-achievers, to replace the school sixth form, to provide specialist and job-orientated skills for people in transition from school to work, to provide broad FE opportunities including O and A levels, to cater for people make a transition from formal education to the real world of providing skills and needs for the wider community. (Industrial Training Officer, ex-Local Authority)

The CFE's function is to promote learning in all its forms for those beyond compulsory school-leaving age. After that it depends on the local situation. I can't be more precise. (DES Official)

Such definitions have their attractions: if we stand far enough away from any problem, it will eventually be dwarfed by the landscape. When we can no longer see the problem, it belongs to someone else. Others can devise mechanisms for defining 'community needs', for getting 'the employers and the population together' to determine their needs. The community solution also fails to justify the by now familiar CFE search for overseas students: how do Nigeria, Hong Kong, Malaysia and Libya fit into the 'local' community of a British college? Clearly what is required is a global view. Only one respondent, obviously accustomed to circumventing the issues, provided a nearly comprehensive answer, carefully dictated from an organisation document:

The college is there to provide education and qualifications to suit industrial, social and education needs at individual, local, national and international (EEC) levels. (CGLI Officer) in which only 'EEC' might be regarded by some colleges as needlessly constraining. So majesterial a perspective is, perhaps, possible only for a validating body officer surveying the scene from Britannia Street. At the interface between the college and the 'local' community, the education-/training issues remain the source of considerable unresolved conflict. Is the college there to serve or to sell? If it can frequently sell by serving, and even serve by selling, what does it do when the two become incompatible? Would you want your son/daughter to marry/'live in' with a missionary? or a marketeer? For most of our respondents, the dilemma appeared to have resulted in an uncomfortable ambivalence, an awareness of competing claims which will not admit of easy resolution.

Summary

One may detect in industry/CFE relationships, and in the rhetoric of the current debate about college responsiveness to industrial need, a number of underlying dichotomies: training and education, preparation for work and self-development, immediate and long-term needs/ends -what has been characterised as the concerns of the marketeer and the missionary. While it is possible for varied concerns to be encompassed within a single training/education programme, there is also implicit in the notions of priority and proportion, the potential for conflict. When the provider and the client disagree, who gets preference, and who decides? A small group of our respondents expressed a clear commitment to one or other of possibly competing demands, but the overwhelming majority sought to accommodate all such demands, differing, however, in their priorities, and in so doing suggesting something of unease and ambivalence.

Chapter 3

PROACTIVE OR REACTIVE: WHAT IS A RESPONSIVE COLLEGE?

The phrase 'the responsive college' was handed to the research team at an early stage by FESC's Director, Geoffrey Melling. He had conceived it as an appropriate title for the staff college's national action programme concerned to raise the level of college responsiveness to the needs of both industry/commerce and individuals, and he had clearly intended it to suggest an institution both proactive and reactive. The OED is not altogether accommodating. It defines *response* as 'an answer, a reply, an action or feeling which answers to some stimulus or influence'; it defines *responsive* as answering, responding, making answer or reply or 'responding readily to some influence'. Roget links *response* with 'answer, reply' and *responsive* with 'impressionable, alive to'. Therefore, responsiveness, by definition, is not an initiating activity. To be responsive is to be reactive, not proactive. As one of our respondents put it,

> . . . A responsive college is one that is less proactive and more reactive. (Industrial Training Officer)

The responsive college will not seek to stimulate demand, but to meet/supply demand, at least in the strict dictionary sense. Of course, a college may be both responsive and proactive at different/the same times, and in different ways. Nevertheless, there is an additional dichotomy here, and one which emerges also in the familiar **Competence and competition** (NEDC/MSC,1984) injunction (my italics):

> Colleges should go to their potential customers with the offer of providing for their needs and wishes at times and in ways which suit the individual. They should *market* rather then *sell*, and, *make customers welcome* on their own terms rather than *pressing them* into college convenience.

To some extent the difficulty is resolved by suggesting that what colleges ought to be selling is their services rather than their products, but even so the resolution does not altogether hold. Marketing includes selling, as the Audit Commission (1985) has subsequently made clear:

> Marketing covers both the assessment of short-term and long-term need and the 'selling' of education and training opportunities to students and prospective employers.

Marketeers do not merely 'read' markets, or go out to discover what local needs are. They also manipulate and create markets: it is difficult to believe that hula hoops and chewing gum originated as responses to articulated community need. The advertising industry exists, at any rate in part, to stimulate demand by arousing acquisitive desires or competitive urges, or both. Marketeers also repackage/advertise to off-load surplus requirements. A marketing college might well be 'selling' courses intended to develop skills for which there was no demand among employers, in which case, of course, it would not be responsive, but it would certainly be proactive.

The difficulty is partly that language is rarely used precisely, and partly that words acquire extended meanings which may not be totally acceptable. What is intended, I would suggest, both by the phrase 'the responsive college' and by the call to marketing among those currently urging colleges to meet employer needs more fully is that colleges should subordinate their own staff needs to those of their clients, that they should be proactive in seeking to identify employer needs, and self-sacrificing with regard to their own interests; or, to put it another way, that they should redefine those interests in terms of employer needs. What is advocated is, once again and paradoxically, an uneasy mixture of the missionary and the marketeer. Something similar is urged in the Audit Commission's **Obtaining better value from further education** (1985) which effectively asks that college staff work harder (larger classes, more classes taught less often, fuller timetables) for less pay (reduced remission, less 'over-grading of staff') so as to free them to 'market' their services more effectively, with an implied end of working still harder for even less pay. It would be interesting to attempt selling the idea to industry/commerce. What we have is selected aspects of the missionary (self-sacrifice) and the marketeer (hustling) approaches placed side by side without any acknowledgement that each derives from a different value system, and that they fit together uncomfortably. To be sure, this latest coupling does no more than reflect the underlying discrepancies and inconsistencies in CFE attitudes to industry/commerce, the attack on materialism and the resentment of reduced resourcing levels. Something of the resultant confusion can be detected in at least a part of our respondents' replies to the question: What is a responsive college?

> It means one that is not rigid, so that it is flexible in changing, proactive rather than reactive. It may be looking five years ahead. (Assistant Head of Industrial Training, Nationalised Industry)

> Responsiveness is a reactive concept, yet colleges are innovative. (NATFHE Officer)

> I haven't heard it myself until your telephone call, but it is useful, and I've used it myself. It indicates reactive rather the proactive. (Chamber of Commerce Officer)

A responsive college is about liaison . . . The characteristics of a responsive college would be culture, awareness, proactive, sensitivity to needs. (Labour MP)

The largest proportion of our respondents saw college responsiveness in missionary terms, as self-sacrifice and the subordination of self-interest to the advantage of others, although there was considerable disagreement about who those others were:

One which is willing to listen to expressed needs and views about change and one where people have the authority to respond once the expression of need has been internalised. (Voluntary Organisation Researcher)

A college that goes out to industry and commerce and listens to industry and commerce, and in doing so surpresses its own preferences, what it wants to do, so as to give priority to industry. (Chief Education Officer)

A college that reacts positively to ascertained and perceived needs of the community in which it is placed, rather than the job market and the needs of employers. It must take account of the needs of the community. (MSC Officer)

A college which is responsive to and aware of the demands of employers . . . That's what we think of as responsive. We recognise that we're not concerned with the whole range of responsiveness, but people misunderstand . . . (MSC Officer)

A college with an effective network of contacts with appropriate customers, not just local industry and commerce. I expect it to have done something radical about mechanical engineering (shut it down), to find it thriving in information technology. I hope to find it has gone out of its way regarding open learning, but not in all areas; that it's handling YTS effectively, despite disputes. (DES Official)

A college that responds to client needs. There are two essential groups: individuals, traditionally 16-19, but now also the adult unemployed, and organisations, most often companies, sometimes the MSC. (Assistant Education Officer)

One that sets out to ascertain and meet what industrial and student need is. (BTEC Officer)

I would guess . . . that it is the difference between a college offering a 'menu' of courses and a college integrated into national needs and responding to users . . . (Industrial Training Officer)

It means responsiveness to the community as a whole. It must include employers, but also the needs of students and trainees as people. Nowadays it means virtually the whole population: ethnic minorities, women, other groups . . . (DES Official)

A college that is conscious of whom it is serving, students, and where they are going (industry or HE), and acknowledges this by designating staff and arranging meetings to discuss these issues (SDP Spokesperson)

We start with the needs of individuals, rather than employers; but they do overlap. I don't see the responsive college as one avidly responding to industry and ignoring individuals. The responsive college should respond in terms of access, i.e. respond to the needs of the unemployed, and consider the length of courses and overcome the 21-hour rule . . . also attract women and ethnic groups. (TUC Officer)

A responsive college gets alongside the customer to identify what he needs to buy. At the moment CFEs are selling what is convenient. (Employers Federation Officer)

A college with new ideas. How receptive are they? For 'idea' you can read kind of course, financial package, etc. (ITB Officer)

A CFE that is concerned to know our particular needs and take account of what organisations say to them, rather than being led by the college. (LA Training Officer)

In the midst of all these encomiums to the virtues of client-centredness, we might well ask what evidence of comparable behaviour can be noted in other British service industries. Solicitors, bankers, shops, hairdressers, trains, estate agents, dentists, hotels and restaurants: how far are they client-centred as distinct from provider-centred? Of course, if they are not, it does not necessarily follow that they are thus regarded as acceptable.

In order to check attitudes to college responsiveness, we put the same question negatively. What distinguishes the non-responsive college? A small group of respondents saw self-interest as a defining characteristic:

Some colleges take the easy way out. They take on full-time students as an easy option. It's hard work for staff liaising with industry, putting on short courses, and it's not doing much for the SSR. (Principal)

One that produces a curriculum to suit itself and doesn't vary it. (Industrial Trainer)

Getting people over fifty to do new things isn't easy with retirement available at fifty-five. (BTEC Regional Co-ordinator)

A nearly similar number saw change/no change as indicative of the responsive/non-responsive college:

It might be a specialist college meeting the explicit needs of industry, but not meeting new needs and doing nothing to change. (SDP Spokesperson)

By and large it could be a relatively small college with a regular supply of students. (BTEC Officer)

Some CFEs 'find' regulations to prevent them from moving, but there are ways around regulations. (Industrial Trainer)

One with a lack of observable initiative. (FEU Officer)

Others saw non-responsiveness as occasioned by inadequate individuals:

Non-responsive colleges have nothing in common except possibly people who are not particularly responsive or who patently believe the old approach was right and the new approaches are unacceptable; and teachers who see industrial training as 'infradig' and who regard repeating the same operations as anathema. (ITB Officer)

It's the calibre of people: no confidence in their own ability, and avoiding the risk of failure. (Industrial Trainer)

We have a more responsive 'system' than anywhere else in the world in systems terms. In pedagogy and delivery we have one of the most conservative teaching forces. It insists on teaching classes, not individuals . . . We have out-of-date equipment, worn-out experts, disgruntled staff. (CGLI Officer)

Or as, at least in part, a consequence of the larger situation:

It's got a dull principal with few ideas, a poor market for its products, and a poor market to draw on for students. It's in an area which is static and stable. They're still doing what they were doing twenty years ago. The staff have dull and non-responsive attitudes of mind. The staff are static. Some of the worst are in X. (HMI)

Those who are under-resourced regarding accommodation, equipment, and staff development, with a lowering of morale. Responsiveness depends on who's judging. (Deputy Education Officer)

For at least one respondent the non-responsive college was only too depressingly familiar:

The unresponsive college is tied to RSA, BTEC, O/A levels

primarily . . . There are only two governors from industry. The advisory committees are filled with personnel clerks. The college has a pompous, ageing principal who is anti-industry and talks about the 'whole person' and 'bull' of that kind. The college isn't open a third of the year. You're unable to reach anybody on the telephone. The brochure has been the same for ten years. The staff are without industrial or commercial experience during the last ten years, except for the lady who runs the typing course. (CBI Officer)

A small number of respondents chose to put responsiveness within a larger environmental context:

A responsive college is one which is sufficiently flexible and innovative to be able to respond to 'turbulence' within the community or industry and commerce . . . and also meet the needs that turbulence throws up (individual or group). (LEA Senior Adviser)

You need a responsive local authority, unless you privatise the college and submit it to full market forces. Local authority services need to be seen as a whole piece. (MSC Officer)

One has to talk about the responsive college within a responsive system: validating bodies, employers accepting what comes out . . . And it's not just content, but style, access, timing. (MSC Officer)

Interviewing does not always produce tidy answers. Some individuals chose to challenge the questions we put to them, or to turn them around to make unexpected points:

Responsiveness means short term. Short term means chaos. Chaos is the inevitable condition of responsiveness. (CGLI Officer)

There is no such thing as a responsive college. There are only people who respond to stimuli. It's the strength of the stimulus which is the major factor determining the speed and quality of response. There's a time factor in responses. FE has 'in the end' responded to every stimulus, but sometimes with a time lag. (Educational Consultant)

One point which virtually no one challenged was whether a college can be responsive or non-responsive, not merely in terms of the implied reification (as questioned in the previous quotation), but in terms of consistency across the whole institution, individual by individual.

Colleges are not always uniformly responsive. They can vary from department to department. Departments with traditional work are not especially responsive to anything except changes to traditional regulations. On the other hand, there are new departments or departments which have gone through hard times and become dependent on a responsive approach. (DES Official)

In fairness, we must acknowledge that most of our respondents were much too polite to query any assumptions embedded in our questions. Later, in responding to requests to identify responsive colleges, many of our interviewees did point to parts of colleges rather then whole institutions. However, the observations in the last quotation call for some amplification. The individuals who make up college staffs are themselves exceedingly varied in terms of:

1. hierarchical rank/status (e.g. Lecturer 1, Principal Lecturer, Head of Department);

2. discipline culture (e.g. engineering, art, sociology, catering);

3. teaching levels (AFE/NAFE, award/non-award bearing);

4. site(s) where teaching takes place;

5. sectional/departmental FT/PT proportions;

6. political commitments;

7. background and qualifications, including industrial/commercial experience;

8. teaching load, including overtime and extra-institutional commitments;

9. relationships with others in the section/department.

In addition, the external environment for which the individual is preparing students can be equally varied:

1. What is the likely employment takeup of student leavers?

2. Does the teacher work with/for local employers, or compete with them?

3. How are the teacher's students regarded by employers?

4. What kind of student demand exists for the teacher's courses?

One need proceed no further with the analysis to perceive that a large number of variables are likely to impinge on responsiveness, and to differ from individual to individual, and from one section/department to another. Moreover, over a period of time, any one individual/section/department is likely to achieve varying levels of responsiveness. At the same time, apart from the teacher and the context, there is also the question of to whom/what he is responding, as several of our respondents pointed out.

> In the end, it's a question of responsiveness to whom. (FEU Officer)

> It's a jargon phrase, so it means nothing, but I assume it means responsive to demand, whatever that may mean. (ITB Officer)

Summary

In strict dictionary sense, responsive represents a reactive (rather than a proactive) activity, but in both the literature and among our respondents there was some disagreement about the extent to which a responsive college could/should initiate activity. However, most of our respondents were agreed that responsive colleges were those which put client interests above provider interests, without ever concurring widely about who those clients actually were. When it came to characterising the non-responsive college, there appeared to be less recognition of provider-centredness and a tendency to identify institutional deficiencies: little evidence of change, poor staff, bad management, inadequate resourcing, unsupportive LEAs. Few respondents questioned the reification implicit in the notion of a responsive college, or wished to advance the idea that responsiveness might vary across a college from individual to individual, course to course, and time to time.

Chapter 4

CONFLICTING INTERESTS: TO WHOM IS A RESPONSIVE COLLEGE RESPONDING?

For an individual lecturer, clients - those who make demands upon the college - might be most usefully conceived as:

1. **primary clients,** i.e. students, those who receive education/training within the college (or the workplace);

2. **secondary clients,** those who perceive themselves as acting as agents for primary clients, whose education/training activities such secondary clients **either**

a) **resource:** (government, MSC; local authorities; parents; students themselves; etc.), **and/or**

b) **legitimise:** (validating/examining agencies/boards; professional bodies; employers; HMI; ITBs; etc.), **and/or**

c) **utilise/or seek to utilise:** (employers; other education/training institutions; ex-students seeking to sell their skills in the market-place; lecturers trying to change society by altering student attitudes/outlooks/-values; etc.).

In the British system, secondary clients can generally be said to be more demanding than primary clients, or at least secondary clients may expect to have their demands confronted more seriously for a number of reasons:

1. In most cases, the NAFE student is not totally 'working his way through college' or borrowing money to pay for his training/education. He can generally expect grants/employers to pay for him, so that he is not a direct purchaser. Most of us are more critical of what we have worked for and bought ourselves, even though we may have (or possibly will have) actually paid towards state subsidy. Therefore the British student tends to be less aggressively consumerist in his approach to learning than many of his European or North American counterparts.

2. NAFE tends to be resourced almost wholly from secondary client groups, who are in turn, highly supportive of the piper/tune adage. The current chorus of 'value for money' is being sung by secondary clients.

3. Secondary clients claim to be acting altruistically for primary clients. The underlying attitude is paternalistic. Inevitably there is a continuing

29

disagreement among secondary client groups as to where the best interests of primary clients lie, but the rhetoric employed in debate tends to suggest disinterested selflessness on the part of secondary clients. Of course, it is almost invariably the case that what is advanced as potentially beneficial for primary clients is generally potentially beneficial for the involved secondary client group. The politics of NAFE tend to be conducted among secondary clients.

We therefore thought it important to attempt to determine our respondents' attitudes towards the whole range of client groups. Because they were broad and general in their framing, the first two questions might be said to have allowed our interviewees to circumvent what we might regard as the central issue: in the politics of NAFE, which group(s) do you back? Or, more specifically, in a conflict, who can expect your support? The question we put to respondents was very specific and contained a number of related parts: To whom should the college be responding? We identified a dozen groups (drawn from the primary/secondary conceptualisation above): students, government, HMI, MSC, local authorities, parents, employers, validating and examining bodies/agencies, professional bodies, ITBs, teachers. We then asked what the college ought to do in the event of disagreement among and within client groups, and which group(s) the respondent would rank as most/least important. A number (more than one in eight) of our respondents would offer no distinctions:

> It depends on the college's priorities. Perhaps all in turn. The college will be influenced by the paymaster. The problem is to identify priorities. (Industrial Trainer)

> I'm concerned about all. (College Principal)

> My concern about the list of clients is that it is over simplistic: the network is more complex. (Senior Adviser)

> Each in his own way. (CGLI Officer)

> All, as far as can be attained. (BTEC Officer)

> It has to respond to the lot. (MSC Officer)

> All in different ways at different levels. (HMI)

Later, some of the above respondents dropped their guard and confronted the issues more directly. For them and others, underlying tensions were discernible. For example, validating bodies seemed to have little support:

> Validating bodies? I wouldn't ask them. We decide and than give them the validation problem. Validating bodies are trivial. (Industrial Trainer)

30

The CFE should be accountable in quality. The question is who are validating bodies accountable to? (Deputy Education Officer)

Validating bodies are immaterial. They are just facilitators. (ITB Officer)

Validating bodies have influence, but our primary concern should be with the customers. (CBI Officer)

My immediate thought is to put validating bodies at the bottom of the list. (ITB Officer)

CFEs respond too much to validation bodies . . . They have no divine right. They are a cabal which needs sorting out. There are too many examination bodies. They should collaborate and be supervised by a corporate body of special partners. Also professional bodies are entrenched and conservative regarding their qualification requirements. (Deputy Education Officer)

I'd put validating bodies at the bottom of the list. They are there to service the other groups. They shouldn't have a vested interest. If they did, I would wonder what role they were playing. All the other groups have legitimate vested interests. (Industrial Training Officer)

At the bottom would be validation bodies. I have a view that there ought to be a single council looking at assessment and standards, means of delivery and content, and the providers should determine how the client gets there. (Senior Adviser)

The last two respondents would doubtless welcome the activities of an MSC/DES Review of Vocational Qualifications Working Group set up by the Secretary of State to

. . . recommend a structure of vocational qualifications in England and Wales which is more responsive and flexible, more accessible and understandable, and provides wider opportunities more relevant to current needs . . .

The Working Group (MSC/DES, 1985) is to issue a final report in 1986.

Apart from validating body employees a single respondent came to the defence of these beleaguered bodies:

Validating bodies help to accommodate more than one client's needs. (Local Authority Training Officer)

There was initially no one to speak up for parents:

Perhaps parents should be at the bottom, although I am loathe to do that. (Industrial Trainer)

Parents would be near the bottom if we see NAFE as post-16 . . . How do we get parents' views? We might respond, yes, but what mechanism is there? (NATFHE Officer)

I would put parents at the bottom. (BTEC Officer)

except in special circumstances:

The clients are at least partly the parents, for example in the case of handicapped students. (DES Official)

A number of secondary client groups drew very little comment:

professional bodies:

It depends on the type of college. Professional bodies are not all that much of a concern in FE. (BTEC Regional Coordinator)

All the groups have power. All influence the life chances of students, even professional bodies . . . HMI reports on professional bodies confirm one's worst prejudices. (DES Official)

industry training boards:

I placed £2,500,000 of contracts with YTS: I will have a purge. The question is: do we think we are getting value for money? (ITB Officer)

local authorities:

It depends on the ethos of the college. If it's a tertiary college, it might be different from a main stream vocational college. You have to know the college role as determined by the LEA and mediated by governors. (FEU Officer)

The college and the LEA are from the same root stock, so you get educational stroking. Insularity is a problem. (Industrial Training Development Officer)

the inspectorate:

There is a moral dilemma, I am sure, about the HMI, but if you define 'client' narrowly, HMI are quality control. (Deputy Staff Manager, Nationalised Industry)

Teachers drew only slightly more comment:

Teachers: you have to work with them. It's extremely important. (BTEC Regional Coordinator)

Teachers? No, because their conditions of service are too liberal. They have an easy time. (ITB Officer and ex-college lecturer)

Approximately a quarter (twelve) of our respondents came down unequivocally on the side of students as the most important client group, although there was not necessarily agreement about how the college might best respond to the student. Four respondents regarded helping the student to employment as a primary concern:

> The employer is a client in so far as he offers employment, but our duty is to the student. Good relations with industry could lead to a job. (Head of Department)

> When the crunch comes, I would support the student. I see the college as part of an educational process. The student is not perfectly informed of the market. The choice of the student is most important. (DES Official)

> Most important are the students because government, HMI, MSC, and LEAs should be responding to what students need rather than what they want, e.g. job-related training rather than arts courses. (ITB Officer)

> The priority should be students requiring qualifications (not necessarily formal) to enable them to do work of a particular kind. This is more than vocational, but it should be job or skill specific. (Industrial Trainer)

Two respondents (the first previously quoted in full) were eager to oppose the primacy of the need-for-jobs argument.

> . . . I would have to say that the priority is offering a general education for life. If you can't afford both this and training for industry and commerce, then the 'purity of life argument' comes first. (Director of Education)

> The individual walking through the door shouldn't be seen as a unit of employment: that would be terrible! We shouldn't assume that the person wants a trade. There has to be room for a person who wants to broaden his skills or talents. (Industrial Training Development Officer)

One individual attempted to accommodate both views:

> The college should be responding to two groups: job training and the unemployed. (ITB Officer)

Five respondents avoided the education/training dilemma altogether by choosing not to qualify their response:

> Students. (BTEC Officer)

> Students. All the rest are secondary. (MSC Officer)

The top priority is young people. You only go 'around the track' once, so use CFEs for young people. There is plenty of time to go through to 9-to-5 and mortgages, etc. (Conservative MP)

The student. Try and conciliate, but put the student first. (Labour MP)

The learners are the priority. (SDP Spokesperson)

One respondent, a principal, found it difficult to conceive of students as individuals, since the college provided for classes *en masse:*

Strangely enough, I would put students at the bottom. Their minds are made up for them. I don't quite know how we react to students. If enough came along, we'd put on a course. We don't do AE. We don't have to react to non-vocational demands.

Two industrialists saw the college primarily in terms of meeting employer needs:

The CFE is an 'arm' of employers. (Deputy Staff Manager, Nationalised Industry)

Employers pay via the rates and taxes. Therefore employers should get what they want. (Employers Federation Officer)

Another group of five respondents attempted to encompass what might be seen as the potentially conflicting demands of students and employers:

Two groups primarily: the individual and the local economy. If we were efficient in this country, it would be the chamber of commerce. (CBI Officer)

There are only two clients: industry and youngsters. All other clients are a means to an end. (Chamber of Commerce Officer)

Students and the local labour market. There is a contradiction which is about specific training, or training for stock. MSC can't accurately predict trends. This is a big argument because MSC aren't prepared to train for stock. We want individual needs back on the agenda. We are losing community education. (NATFHE Officer)

There are only two groups which are important: students and the people for whom they're going to work. (MSC Officer)

Students and employers: they overlap. (LA Training Officer)

A further group of three respondents circumvented the need for distinguishing among groups by the holistic community approach:

> The customer is the community. The college should be serving local needs. (Chamber of Commerce Officer)

> The college is there to meet the educational needs of the locality. It should be responding to the community, servicing the local community. (ITB Officer)

> The college's main accountability is to the community that supports it, to the local authority, and through them to the public generally. (Principal)

At one level, the line of questioning we put to respondents was deliberately simplistic in order to encourage individuals to reveal their underlying loyalties, or at least to expose the commitments they were prepared to make public, which may not be identical with the former. At another level, one could answer the question (to whom?) in terms of *should* (ideal state) and *does* (what happens in the real world). The overwhelming majority of respondents chose the ideal state approach, into which category I would put those responses quoted above, and the three which follow, slightly more extended in analysis because they consider a larger number of groups, but nonetheless centred on what should happen (despite the assertion by the first respondent):

> My ranking would be students, employers and ITBs. I would put validation bodies at the bottom: we 'wag' the C & G. (ITB Officer)

> I would put parents at the bottom after government and validating bodies. (DES Official)

> My priorities would be, in this order, students, local authorities, parents, teachers. I would put validating bodies at the bottom. (Voluntary Organisation Researcher)

Of course, all of the above respondents answered our questions more or less as set (others evaded them altogether). We asked, to whom should . . .? What we received were respondent alignments roughly in favour of students and employers, with some awareness of the potential demands of other client groups, little (although perhaps regretful) interest in parental views and considerable disapprobation directed at validating bodies, clearly the villains of the piece[1]. Yet there is no real necessity to answer any interviewer's question in the way in which it is set out, and a number of our respondents chose to come at the issues in their own ways. Three, for example, took a predominantly 'market' view:

> CFEs respond to people with money in X. They respond to mainly

---

1. Nor surprisingly, respondents were consistent in seeing their own membership groups as important and helpful, rather than the reverse.

16-19 FT, and anyone who has money. (Assistant Education Officer)

Anyone who provides money has control. Teachers have control. Students have little control. (TUC Officer)

It depends on whom you're asking the question. Most colleges respond according to who brings the income. (FEU Officer)

Money is, of course, an important variable and a source of power and authority, but not always the only source. In the real college world, the progress of client group demand and interaction is essentially a political process, a dynamic in which prediction is sometimes difficult. Collectively, another group of respondents noted the additional importance of organisational mission:

It depends on the type of college. There are two extremes. One is the art college which has a special set of demands. Then there is the college which is developing a new curriculum for 16-year-olds, where the constraints are the students themselves, validating bodies, HMI and, increasingly, MSC. One is responding to different demands in the art college and in the college with predominantly 'New FE' students. (FE Inspector)

value systems:

The college will pursue the practice and provision which fits the bill of responding to the most important clients. The college may need to state the top ten sources of responsiveness: 'Our number one client is . . . ' There should be some understanding about which client groups are most important, but colleges do, and will continue to, compromise and be all things to all men. In the college, the principal might respond to one set of messages if he were orchestrating for the British economy, but he might choose another if he were an altruistic principal. (DES Official)

resourcing constraints:

You have to steer carefully between groups. I'm not certain education is unresponsive. It may be slow to respond with its committees and bureaucracy. Colleges have to listen to all sorts of people . . . Colleges may be responsive to someone else's voice. All institutions and management are conservative. If you have a large capital investment and staff in one area, it's not easy to cut it in half immediately . . . (MSC Officer)

effective lobbying:

I believe colleges are very responsive to the messages they really receive, which may not be the messages people think and hope they receive. (DES Official)

immediacy of pressure:

> The college will react to the stimulus which is most powerful at the time ... The college is an echo system, a biological system, like a hedgerow. There's a constant conflict of stimuli, but the colleges are adept at reconciling. The head of department who hasn't the equipment may find the equipment. People who create stimuli don't understand colleges ... Who controls the money is most important . . . There's an interaction between the college's perceptions of what it's there to do and what's being demanded of it. (Educational Consultant)

> It depends on the aims of the college. I would put students at the top, and employers high. Students and employers have needs; others have demands. Parents often want O levels, which can sometimes be the wrong course. You have to compromise: you don't run too far ahead of the market-place. I would put government and HMI at the bottom: they're so far away, which is not to say the college shouldn't respond. It depends . . . on the context. Response is a broad term. (HMI)

and sheer 'clout':

> I wouldn't put anybody at the bottom of the list, but I bet colleges would. We have found in colleges a fairly low opinion of HMI and local authorities. The MSC came from Moorfoot to give a questionnaire. BTEC came out high as a major influence . . . (FE Inspector)

which suggests that the gap between what is considered desirable and what actually occurs may be exceptionally wide, a possibility supported by the DES/HMI **Education for employees** (1984a):

> . . . too many teachers assume that validating bodies have prescribed aims and methods ... Validating bodies often do give the impression of being prescriptive: they may not set out to prevent initiative but they do very little to encourage it . . . employers and colleges need to be clear about what each can best deliver and make a more determined effort to use work settings as the base for learning . . .

While it might be argued that the majority of our respondents failed to delineate the complexities of the political[2] process through which client

2. The few who did mention 'political' did not elaborate, but allowed the word to carry its own unspoken reverberations. 'If there is disagreement, this is a political issue'. (Industrial Training Officer).

group conflicts are resolved because our questioning required them to simplify, I would point to the last eight quotations which offer interesting analyses of the interaction process. Moreover, in another question, we asked respondents to confront the conflict issue head on: How does the college deal with conflict among competing client demands? The responses suggested that for a significant proportion of our respondents political conflict, at least at the level of public acknowledgement, was barely discernible. One respondent viewed it as a novelty:

> I've not had much experience of such conflicts. (Principal)

another doubted its existence:

> We wouldn't accept that being responsive to one is at the expense of another. Responding to student needs can also relate to other needs. (NATFHE Officer)

a third advocated pleasing some of the people some of the time:

> Being cynical, at the moment CFEs cater to validating bodies, staff, and administrative convenience, the easy life . . . but if there are conflicting demands, the college should respond to a variety of clients rather than by 'ranking' clients. (Industrial Training Officer)

Approximately a third of our respondents offered what one may describe as a mechanistic solution to conflict:

1. **Refer the problem upwards,** although there was disagreement about where the 'buck' would stop:

a) **the principal:**
> If you have a tough, dynamic, executive-style principal, he will make the decision and get backing. (Industrial Trainer)

b) **the governing body:**
> The college is part of a total service. Elected members do a difficult job. They have the right to set priorities. We can argue with them, but we can't ignore them. (Principal)

> There should be room for meeting different requirements. The governing body should be operating as a board in a company. The college should use the board to set long-term strategy. (CBI Officer)

> The governing body and advisory groups should help to overcome conflict. There's not so much conflict if the college is involved in the community and has the involvement of the community. (ITB Officer)

c) **the local authority:**

If there is disagreement or a simple polarity, the college has to seek the advice of the non-involved partner and look to meditation. (FE Inspector)

The LEA has to decide. That is their job. (Industrial Trainer)

We're talking about the politics of the institution. The CFE is a public body, so the LEA sets up priorities in the light of the Government's guidelines. (SDP Spokesperson)

It's not for the colleges to decide in every case, but for the LEA to decide. (DES Official)

d) **b) and c) together:**

The governing body and the LEA have to become more centrally involved in planning colleges. This goes against the autonomy of colleges, which is not relevant to turbulence. (Senior Adviser)

One respondent warned of the dangers of referring upwards for a decision:

Disagreement? We have those problems . . . You have to assess the best one, and then convince people . . . If you're not willing to make decisions, but are inclined to push it up to someone else, where do you stop? Sir Keith? (Industrial Trainer)

2. **Leave it to the market:**

I don't see any problems. The real problem is whether the price is right. (MSC Officer)

The CFEs should choose the industry which is going to pay most. (Chamber of Commerce Officer)

If I were a principal, I would have to ask about the resources available and the philosophy underlying provision. It is very complex. Money is an issue. Is the industry growing or declining? (ITB Officer)

I don't see colleges as in a different position from commercial enterprises. They should look at threats and opportunities. They're in the market-place. Whatever you do will upset somebody. If I were a college, I'd want to maintain the broadest possible clientele. At the end of the day, I'd have to recognise that the chap with money is the chap I've got to go for. (ITB Officer)

If there is disagreement, choose the one which gives the best return as the college perceives it. (Deputy Staff Manager, Nationalised Industry)

One respondent acknowledged the power of the market somewhat reluctantly:

> In today's economic climate, money plays a large part. The college is there for students, and it involves all sorts of people, but it's easy to lose sight of students. (BTEC Regional Coordinator)

3. Reorganise the college:

> If there is disagreement in the college, get rid of inter-departmental boundaries. But I don't mean introduce a matrix system: they never work. But introduce a Director of Studies with VP status who can knock heads together. (ITB Officer)

One respondent saw the solution to conflict in prioritising:

> The college has to determine priorities, but they cannot be permanent because demands change. (Educational Consultant)

and two revealed where their priorities would lie:

> If the client is big enough, CFEs should respond ... although there is a convenience factor. (Chamber of Commerce Officer)

> You have to respond to employers if you want students to get jobs. At the moment we have the ideas of teachers taking over. Students learn skills they may never use. (ITB Officer)

and a fourth saw the act of prioritising as an issue of professional competence:

> There are very limited numbers of important significant interests. There will be inputs from a whole range of bodies. It's a test of the competence of staff separating wheat from chaff. (MSC Officer)

and a similar commitment to the notion of rational beings collectively agreeing rational solutions underlay the advocacy of negotiation by five other respondents:

> You have to solve conflict by negotiation, sometimes hitting middle ground, sometimes discarding views. (HMI)

> If there are two choices, you can adopt both, or choose, or try to reconcile them. (Educational Consultant)

> If there is disagreement among client groups, then they should hold joint consultative meetings and 'table' points of view and come up with conglomerate needs and work towards a compromise. This could be a basic course for all, and then specialist courses. (Deputy Head, Nationalised Industry)

> Some system of priority is needed, but it is difficult to order them. But there is a method of setting priorities: by negotiation. (TUC Officer)

> CFEs must recognise that advice comes from different directions . . . Through discussion, they have to try and get consensus. (Director of Education)

No such consensus could be said to have existed among our respondents with regard to the priorities to be advocated or identified among the potentially conflicting demands of the college's client groups. We could hardly have expected otherwise. Our respondents themselves are representatives of different client groups and it is at the point where their own demands fail to converge that differences are likely to surface. Prioritising (or refusing to do so publicly) among client groups is itself part of the political process, a fact to which one of our respondents made clear reference:

> Responsiveness can lead to conflict . . . This happened with X polytechnic. They want it their way and just take the cash . . . so now they are defensive. (LA Training Officer)

However, in the real world, client groups are seldom equally resourced. Ultimately the views of parents are likely to be subordinate to those of the local authority, and those of local authority officers to those of validating bodies: in conflict situations, some combatants are better armed than others. It is therefore interesting to observe how infrequently MSC has appeared in the preceding pages, despite the fact that the whole responsiveness debate (and this project, with its interviews, which forms a part of that debate) has been triggered off by **Training for jobs, Competence and competition,** the twenty-five per cent NAFE takeover, and the MSC/LAA compromise for local development plans. A stranger to these shores reading through the foregoing quotations would be hard pressed to idenify MSC as an important and influential client group, while at the same time it is difficult to think of any other client group (apart from central government) which has more successfully forced its demands through the FE system, despite the protests of gatekeepers such as LEAs. There is clearly a paradox. Among our respondents, only four placed MSC centrally in replying to the basic question: To whom is a responsive college responding? One, an MSC Officer, put the 'firm's view' somewhat apologetically:

> I would put the emphasis on job prospects and employment, I accept the rest also . . . but I focus on employment. It's not a sophisticated view. It's not about education.

The remaining were more explicit:

Many colleges are responding to MSC because there's money there. I'm not sure it's a valid reason. (BTEC Regional Coordinator)

I put MSC at the top. (Principal)

I put the weight on MSC. No, that's not correct: not MSC, but on employment . . . on the issues of employment and changing employment . . . Have you got my correction? (MSC Officer)

Summary

We postulated a dozen primary and secondary client groups who might be seen as directing demands towards colleges and asked our respondents to consider the claims of, and priorities among, the groups. Approximately a fifth of our respondents chose to make no distinctions, either by insisting that they would wish to respond to all demands, or by suggesting that CFEs ought to be concerned with the community as a totality. A nearly similar proportion suggested that students were the most important client group, without agreeing about what student needs were; and smaller proportions gave preference to employers (less than one per cent) or both students and employers (nearly a tenth, although without necessarily distinguishing relative importance). Thus, just over a third concentrated on employers/students, the groups whose needs the largest proportion of our respondents were prepared to champion.

Other client groups fared less well. More than a sixth of our respondents perceived validating bodies as having no legitimate demands to which colleges might be expected to respond. Nine other secondary client groups found either few (parents, professional bodies, ITBs, LEAs, HMI, teachers, MSC) or no (government, examining bodies) supporters among our respondents.

More than a fifth of our interviewees attributed relative importance among client groups to the influence of contextual variables: the persuasive power of money, organisational mission, cultural values, resourcing constraints, effective lobbying, organisational support.

With reference to how the college might resolve conflicting/competing client group demands, the solutions favoured among our respondents might be described as mechanistic (referring problems upwards, trusting the market, reorganising the college), rational (thinking it through), and consensual (discussion, negotation).

Chapter 5

COLLEGE RESPONSIVENESS: CHARACTERISTICS AND CONSTRAINTS

At an early stage of this project, we looked forward to identifying a limited number of colleges widely regarded as responsive, with a view to locating, after Peters/Waterman's **In search of excellence,** a group of defining characteristics. It rapidly became apparent that no such identification would occur. Some of our respondents (several DES civil servants, validating body central officers) were far too removed from the individual college level to be able to name distinguished institutions. Others (validating and ITB regional officers) knew only some colleges in particular parts of the country. Industrial trainers generally had contacts with only local CFEs. Moreover, for many of these respondents, 'the college' meant one or two departments. Although some respondents did have a national perspective from which to provide us with names, collectively our interviewees were drawing upon varied data bases, ranging, in compass, from nil to the nation. Consequently we limited the intended scope of our research.

Of our 54 respondents, 16 declined/were unable to name any college (or part thereof) as being particularly responsive. One DES civil servant replied, 'I'm at a loss. Ask the HMIs!' The remaining 38 respondents offered us the names of 80 colleges in England, Scotland and Wales, the largest group (13) naming only one institution and one individual providing a list of nine colleges. Fifteen colleges were named twice, and four on three occasions, but one of the latter colleges had been the previous employer of two respondents who brought it to our attention. Two of our principals assured us that their colleges were uniformly responsive in all areas, although one conceded that there might be 'marginal' differences among departments.

We turned next to trying to get respondents to identify the source of responsiveness: What distinguishes the responsive college? Could its achievements be attributable to individuals, the way it organised itself (structures), something about its situation/setting (declining rolls, fierce competition), or some combination of the foregoing?

The smallest group (nine) saw structures as important. Several respondents offered some kind of amplification:

A matrix structure allows management to be spread amongst senior staff. (Chamber of Commerce Officer)

Management structure helps in terms of indicating whom to approach. (LA Training Officer)

but in most instances structures were included in the answer 'all', without any further comment being offered[1].

Eleven respondents regarded situation/setting as crucial, although there was general agreement that the 'survival instinct' did not always surface when survival was at stake.

> The context is important. Whether people have their backs to the wall, whether there's an influx of new industry and resulting opportunities: those things are important. They are things that staff respond to. It doesn't always happen, but in many cases it does.(MSC Officer)

> The scene is set by socio-economic factors and action is necessary, but when and the form are determined by individuals.(Educational Consultant)

One MSC Officer pointed out that having its back to the wall had not always been a stimulus to survival in British Industry. Another respondent, from the DES, rejected the notion of context as a determining variable:

> There's nothing in the setting or situation which makes a college responsive. You get responsive colleges in everything from true blue Tory prosperous to embattled recessionary Britain. There is a lot to do with people, with the personalities of managers: the principal, the VP, the heads of department.

A local authority senior adviser saw 'context' in terms of political setting:

> One important characteristic is the degree of conservatism at the political level in LEAs, so that, for example, in FE terms, despite X being Tory controlled, it is more buzzing and exciting than others, reflecting imaginative management at the political level.

By far the largest number of respondents (45) saw personalities and individuals as the crucial determinant in responsiveness. Among these interviewees, 37 literally identified 'personality' as central, while others developed the notion in terms of effective activity: management style, leadership ability, contacts with industry, the capacity to allocate resources appropriately. As to the question of whose personality was instrumental in stimulating (or not) responsiveness, some respondents pointed to vice-principals and heads of department, but the largest number insisted that the principal mattered more than anyone else in the organisation:

> A tough, dynamic, executive-style principal will make decisions and get backing. (Industrial Trainer)

---

1. Seven respondents attributed some importance to each of the three identified variables.

If the principal is good, he can carry people with him. . . A principal must have the ability to shape the college. (Industrial Trainer)

We don't talk to the minors. We talk with the principal. He is the facilitator and can open doors for L2s and SLs. He gives their work legitimacy. (Industrial Trainer)

Principals need 1) leadership and knowledge of potential resources amongst staff, 2) to be entrepreneurial, i.e. outward looking, known to the business world and with an ear to the ground to identify which businesses are useful to the college. (Chamber of Commerce Officer)

The authority went tertiary. This was a good opportunity, yet the principal of X was old fashioned, so no revolutionary transformation took place. A missed opportunity! (Educational Consultant)

The difficulty is that in CFEs and LEAs most principals . . . have got there at a time of expansion and have grown up in different times and have no (or little) imagination and skill to do perhaps what they ought to be doing. (Senior Adviser)

Sometimes colleges are not open enough: principals don't communicate to their staff. (Assistant Education Officer)

The personality and management skills of the principal determine college responsiveness. (MSC Officer)

The fundamental nexus is the principal and the head of department through which processes are modified. Local authorities are unsystematic. Much is left to the principal and his advisers. (DES Official)

If the CFE had a really committed principal, he or she would make it happen, and this would affect college management. Its a matter of an individual's personal philosophy and value system. High achievers will do things at personal risk, or either they leave or 'toe-the-line'. (Industrial Trainer)

In colleges, if you change people - especially the principal - the college can alter significantly. (BTEC Regional Coordinator)

If principals are so central to responsiveness, and responsiveness is so desirable, we might well ask why principals are appointed potentially for the remainder of their working lives. Overseas systems often appoint staff on a 'trial' basis or offer, particularly for heads of institution, fixed-term contracts which can be renewed, or not, as appropriate. The alternative, if principals are the key determinant, involves leaving responsiveness to luck. An HMI argued:

> I would advocate more careful selection of principals, vice-principals, heads.

but only two respondents (a DES civil servant and an MSC officer/ex principal) suggested that fixed-term appointments were advisable:

> Whilst tenure exists, there's precious little that can be done with an inadequate principal. Of course, you can buy them out, but I don't want to see people hired and fired too much . . .(DES Official)

A Chamber of Commerce Officer did not see the principal as the only point at issue:

> Relationships with principals are OK, but disagreement exists within the college at other levels. They are big institutions. It is the same with MSC.

By asking respondents to identify the determinant(s) of responsiveness, and then directing their attention to three specific variables, we could be said to have both focused and constrained their answers. We therefore put two additional questions to them, broader and non-directive in scope, but effectively identical, apart from being put positively and negatively:

1. If you had central (or local) power over a group of colleges, what would you advocate to increase responsiveness?

2. What do you perceive as the main obstacle to responsiveness?

Not all the respondents were able or willing to attempt either or both questions:

> I've never thought about it. FE officers tend to look to principals and senior staff in colleges. I try to encourage my staff. How you get positive responses, I don't know. (Principal)

> I can't answer. It is not always the college which is at fault, as there is not always someone to respond to. (Head of Department)

Some were unwilling to acknowledge a problem:

> I don't know how far colleges are not responsive. I would need to know that. Maybe not all of them have a need to change . . . The way the local authority runs this college is pretty reasonable. They have a hands-off approach. We're the only college in the authority . . . The local authority leaves management to the college. We have flexibility in the use of staff. We ignore conditions of service . . . (Principal)

Nothing. Colleges have had it too good for too long. (BTEC Regional Coordinator)

The MSC/LAA **Report of policy group** (1985) attributes to the FEU the feeling that

> ... the expectations of employers with respect to what could be delivered in curricular terms by standard mainstream vocational courses were often unrealistic.

Within the system we can therefore locate individuals who are prepared to suggest that no problem exists, or that the difficulty is one-sided unreasonableness.

Some of the respondents who answered both questions were not always consistent in seeking to remove perceived constraints. For example, one interviewee advocated increased resourcing, but saw Burnham conditions of service as the principal barrier; another identified uncertainty over resourcing levels as inhibiting, but was concerned primarily to clarify principal and governing body management roles. Nevertheless, the majority of respondents identified constraints which they sought to alleviate, for which reason it will be useful to examine the resultant data in terms of area of perceived difficulty.

At this point our respondents were collectively liberal in locating the blame in virtually every part of the educational system, as well as in industry, the client group whose allegedly unmet needs had prompted our enquiry.

1. **Central Government.** Two respondents (a DES civil servant and an MP) saw responsiveness as inhibited primarily by the split at central government level between education and training. Both argued for a merger.

2. **Local Authorities.** A group of five respondents saw LEAs as the real source of difficulty. An MP felt that, 'Many LEAs need a kick', and a CBI officer suggested that responsiveness could be improved by 'taking colleges from LEAs'. An industrialist argued that college lecturers should be LEA based and should circulate among colleges, as required. An AEO urged that LEAs should be made to 'monitor' FE colleges more assiduously.

3. **Resourcing.** Nineteen individuals regarded resourcing as the key to improved responsiveness. Ten saw colleges as under-resourced. Three wanted either to abolish the fee-paying system or to provide automatic maintenance grants. Six sought to allow colleges greater financial autonomy and/or the right to keep profits:

> We should adopt some of the features of successful businesses, e.g. identify firm remits and cash targets, and give remits to managers and make them personally responsible, rewarding and

chastising them, but freeing them at the same time from restrictions on how to deliver[2]. (Director of Education)

Two AEOs felt that improved resource allocation would stimulate better college performance. An educational consultant wanted to 'abolish most project funding and pump priming' which he regarded as largely wasteful. A principal was highly critical of a current effort to improve college responsiveness:

> PICKUP is a lot of hot air. They have a small budget. They couldn't have done very much . . . It was created at the wrong time: five years after the right idea, ten years after it could have been useful. What PICKUP required was the college I worked in fifteen years ago, which had quite a bit of fat. Colleges are pared to the bone. They need to recruit additional staff.

an explanation expressly contradicted by a Chamber of Commerce Officer:

> Colleges use no money as an excuse, but I don't believe it. It's the L2s, the SLs who determine responsiveness.

4. **Colleges.** The largest number of respondents (24) saw the college as the source of the most serious difficulties.

a) **Location.** An ITB officer regarded the geographical position of some colleges as an obstacle to responsiveness:

> We might want to relocate colleges. X College should not be where it is, but should be in Y.

b) **Staff.** Twenty respondents identified college personnel as the major problem, sometimes alarmingly so:

> There's little incentive for staff. There's a great deal of apprehension and unfamiliarity. They worry about being out of their depth. (DES Official)

There was also concern that long-serving lecturers might be 'burnt out'; other lecturers needed retraining, updated industrial/community experience, or changed attitudes; staff were sometimes personally insecure; principals required 'high grade' support staff, with the gap between principal and registrar perceived as 'too wide'. Upon occasion, individual respondents were specifically prescriptive: seek for 'inspired leadership'; develop 'the ability to say no' so as to avoid undertaking tasks which the college is unable to complete successfully; or (as noted above) employ senior staff on limited tenure contracts. A LA Training Officer pinpointed the source of his frustration:

2. Trial schemes to promote financial autonomy in schools have been attempted in Solihull (Humphrey and Thomas, 1983 and 1983a) and Cambridge (Burgess and Hinds, 1983) with apparent mixtures of advantages/disadvantages. Knight (1983) analyses some of the dangers.

The biggest thing is that heads of department need education in management training. It is 'amateurish', hit and miss at the moment. This extends all the way down the college: failing to attend meetings, failing to fill in forms . . . We haven't been told that students are doing an assignment: they just turn up and I'm not prepared. There is not enough collaboration. I understand why enthusiasm is wanting, but I'm talking about senior staff.

c) **Conditions of Service.** Eight respondents drew attention to what they regarded as Burnham regulation constraints on deploying staff flexibly. One sought to promote greater use of the extended year and another of the extended day.

d) **Accountability.** One respondent wanted to make heads of department accountable for responsiveness; a second wanted a 'simplified system of accountability' which avoided 'interference from many tiers' as resources were channelled from central government to colleges; a third was 'worried' about the education committee's oversight of colleges and the 'political processes at local government level'.

e) **Tradition.** Three respondents saw the past history of education, and the established ways of doing things, as almost insuperable barriers:

The weight of education is so heavy . . . history . . . precedents. (Industrial Trainer)

5. **The curriculum.** Seven respondents pointed to the organisation and content of the curriculum as being a major source of non-responsiveness: 'validating body interests' were inhibiting; the whole system of qualifications needed to be simplified; there should be a single validating council for NAFE; vocational education and training should be restructured on a modular basis and there should be greater reliance on industrial/community 'work-based activities'; the course categorisation system was unhelpful.

6. **Industry.** While a clear majority (33) of respondents saw constraints to responsiveness as lying somewhere in the education/training system, there was a small group (9) who placed the blame elsewhere:

The problems are on the demand rather than the supply side. (DES Official)

The UK doesn't have powerful enough chambers of commerce and trade. No one voice speaks on behalf of the business community. It's a fundamental weakness . . . When X says, 'You employers can't articulate your needs', it hurts. (CBI Officer)

Employers should be educated. (Labour MP)

Employers are the biggest stumbling block, bigger than trades unions. (Chamber of Commerce Officer, ex-ACAS)

There is a need for a local manpower committee that can feed to the Area Manpower Board because there is a gap in knowledge of the manpower scene . . . not a sectoral approach because you get a proliferation of committees, but cross-sector . . . and look for skill shortages locally, probably not above the technician level . . . MSC is getting information, but no one is pulling it together, and MSC should be . . . (Industrial Officer)

Dead beat managers in industry are the real problem. That's over-simplified, of course, but I would put the dead-beat managers ahead of dead-beat college staff. It's within the power of important customers of CFEs to go along to colleges and say, 'You really must improve your performance' . . . If the manager in industry said, 'We must have . . .', other things would fall into place. (MSC Officer)

If you have an old-fashioned (in the context of competitive) industry and training strategy, colleges will be old-fashioned. Colleges can't isolate themselves, including the old-fashioned. (FEU Officer)

Maybe pressure should be put on industry to liaise with colleges. Industry often pays more for private provision. They don't always use college provision well. (BTEC Regional Coordinator)

I accept that employers have a role. It is easy to criticise the CFE. Employers have to be responsive to the college. It's a question of who is responsible. We get the same problem in the County Council: personnel and treasurers can't collaborate. (LA Training Officer)

These final observations bring us again to the larger context on which we have previously only touched. Colleges do not exist in a social and cultural vacuum. Those who have occasion to travel both at home and abroad might well wish to question whether British industry, particularly in its servicing/retailing functions, is genuinely responsive by overseas standards. In British hotels, restaurants, pubs, shops and banks, one might well doubt whether what is offered has been organised primarily to meet the individualised needs of customers, or whether the latter are well and responsively served. To what extent are customers/clients expected to accept what, how and when according to provider requirements? How easily can one obtain a hotel breakfast (which one has often been required to purchase) before 7a.m., or obtain an alcoholic drink/lunch after 2p.m., shop after 6p.m., bank on Saturdays, find sustenance in trains/railway stations after 11p.m.? One might well question whether those college which are perceived as non-responsive in their service function actually stand out dramatically from the general service sector background, or reflect what is also characteristic of the whole provision, the microcosm of the macrocosm. Lecturers, after all, seek as well as provide services, and their attitudes to servicing may be influenced by experiences outside, as well as inside, colleges. Moreover, many of the service industries - including those mentioned above, e.g. hotels, restaurants, banks - have traditionally used CFEs to train their staff. Are there genuinely significant discontinuities in client-centredness across the college/industry boundary? It is interesting that **Competence and competition** does not exhort hoteliers, restaurateurs, and bankers, as well as lecturers, to

> . . . go to their potential customers with the offer of providing for their needs and wishes at times and in ways which suit the individual.

Of course, both competence and competition are relative concepts. If it is essential that effective activity must expand under both headings, there is no easy justification for its not surfacing first in CFEs if we are to break the 'vicious circle'. However, that non-responsiveness may not be a localised affliction, confined predominantly to CFEs, is suggested by those respondents who found cause for concern among employers, as well as colleges. Relationships, even of the client/provider variety, are two-way arrangements.

At the same time, we might note a number of other features of such relationships:

1. There is little likelihood that responsiveness can ever be absolute and total. If one thinks in terms of a continuum with ideal-state responsiveness at one end and ideal-state non-responsiveness at the other, the probability is that all organisations can be located somewhere between the two hypothetical extremes. The absolutely non-responsive college would have no students. The perfectly responsive college is difficult to imagine in this world. In striving for a 'responsive college' one is therefore seeking a more responsive institution: the aim is to move the organisation towards the hypothetical perfect end of the continuum, in which case the argument is one of degree rather than kind, with the point along the continuum, where the intolerable becomes acceptable, like so much else in the world of CFEs, neither defined nor measured.

2. It is possible that the point referred to above can never be located for all by anyone, since everyone will perceive it differently, and that a college can be described as responsive (or not) only with reference to the majority of its clients, which, in turn, would mean that client perceptions may be a function of both demand and expectation.

3. Insofar as demand and expectation may vary from client to client, from area to area (even country to country), and from time to time (demands may change, expectations may rise or fall), responsiveness can have meaning only with reference to particular groups of clients at a given time, i.e. responsiveness has continually to be achieved.

4. In the client-provider relationship, the client holds the upper hand, i.e. the customer is always right[3], since he initiates the demands, carries the expectations and confers the epithet 'responsive'.

5. Responsiveness (or its absence) cannot be solely a function of those clients who arrive, but must also reflect those potential clients who took their demands elsewhere because they had lost any expectation of satisfaction.

If one accepts the above, then the distinguishing characteristics of college responsiveness must lie in a fundamental desire, and an ability, among a significant proportion of college staff to satisfy client demands and expectations, and the evidence of success/failure in terms of responsiveness must lie with clients, rather than in the college or its staff. Of course, constraints may impede and frustrate the desire/ability among the staff, but removing or alleviating such constraints will not necessarily produce either the desire or ability where they do not already exist.

In describing one of the essential characteristics of their excellent companies, Peters/Waterman make the point forcefully:

> A simple summary of what our research uncovered on the customer attribute is this: the excellent companies really are close to their customers. That's it. Other companies talk about it; the excellent do it . . . recent theory talks about the importance of the external environment in influencing the institution. It misses by a mile, however, the intensity of customer orientation that exists within top performers, and that intensity seems to be one of the best kept secrets in American business.

Client-centredness means client-centredness means . . .

3. I discuss the related problems in Chapter 7.

Summary

Our respondents were collectively unable to offer us a group of colleges whose responsiveness had gained widespread acknowledgement: just over 70 per cent of the interviewees advanced the names of 80 institutions perceived as wholly or partly responsive, but no one institution was noted more than three times, and nearly half were named by a single individual. More than 80 per cent of the respondents identified individual personality (especially that of the principal) as the major determinant of college responsiveness, with considerably smaller proportions attributing any significant influence to situation/setting or organisation structure.

When asked how colleges might be made more responsive, respondents offered diverse suggestions spread over virtually the whole spectrum of college system activity, advancing the necessity/desirability of: central government reorganisation; altered LEA activity (losing colleges, appointing staff on an authority basis, monitoring CFEs more effectively); changes in CFE resourcing (more, new financing arrangements, greater financial autonomy); major adjustments to college activity (relocation, better/retrained staff, new conditions of service, greater/clearer accountability, etc.); new reorganised curricula; and similar kinds of changes in industry/commerce.

Finally, with reference to the latter criticisms of industry, it was suggested that education/training, as a service industry, might be neither significantly more nor less responsive than most providers in the same sector (the microcosm/macrocosm); that total and complete responsiveness is unlikely in the real world, since responsiveness exists (or not) within the perceptions of clients, and is therefore a function of expectation/fulfilment, the perception of which may vary from client to client, place to place, and time to time, i.e. responsiveness cannot be either universal or final. Therefore making a college more responsive means moving the institution further along a client perceptual continuum from one hypothetical end/tendency (non-responsiveness) towards its hypothetical opposite.

Chapter 6

CASH OR CONVICTION: SHOULD COLLEGES ADOPT A BUSINESS ETHIC?

In recent years, CFEs have come under increasing pressure to change their alledgedly academic, provider-centred, inefficient and inward-looking ways into something more outgoing, client-centred and commercial in approach. Colleges should be run more like businesses, the argument goes; they should be more competitive, they should generate (at least a part of) their own income, they should increase productivity. From the broadest perspective, one may view such exhortations as part of a wide Western movement towards a marketing philosophy and an attendant assertion that market forces are self-sufficient regulators in any social/commercial setting: markets solve problems better than governments. This is hardly the place to rehearse the arguments for and against, but we need to bear in mind that CFEs have latterly had to conduct their affairs against a background of such arguments, pro and con. The Audit Commission's (1985) main recommendations underscore a by-now familiar message: colleges need to concern themselves with

> Better marketing of further education courses . . . Tailoring teaching resources more closely to demand . . . Better cost recovery . . . Tight control over non-teaching costs . . .

From the present Government's point of view, the promotion of a marketing/business approach in colleges has the virtues of reducing public expenditure (through enhanced efficiency and institutional fund-raising) and supporting political philosophy. There is also an apparently widely held conviction that British education is traditionally and fundamentally anti-commerce/industry. Such a conviction underlies a number of **Competence and competition** (NEDC/MSC, 1984) recommendations:

> The time has come for individuals to see that their desire for learning is relevant to their employment roles . . . Individuals at all levels need to become more conscious of the types of competence in demand in . . . labour markets . . . The education service and media should show individuals the rewards - both economic and qualitative - of reliance on one's own efforts and of using learning at work . . .

However, I would suggest that the depiction of CFEs, and even of education as a whole, as consistently anti-business is a caricature which it is difficult to sustain. In the first place, as the effects of falling rolls have begun to affect organisations (first colleges of education, then schools, and in the near future CFEs), they have increasingly found themselves in competition for survival with one another. In particular, CFEs and polytechnics have in many instances for some time been concerned with revenue-generating activities: the whole range of MSC-sponsored intitiatives - YOP, TOPS, YTS, TVEI, etc.; the production of full-cost short courses; college lettings; consultancy work; running profitable training restaurants and hairdressing salons. Additionally, the effects of the recession and technological developments on industry/commerce, with resulting unemployment, have already forced at least parts of existing CFEs to confront the dilemmas of shrinking traditional markets and the growth of new ones. The answer, therefore, to the question with which we began this chapter is not centred on *should* but on *how far should*. That colleges are often currently involved in commercial enterprises was a point put forcefully by several of our respondents:

> Colleges are entrepreneurial. They do market, determine need and work in interests already in the college (staff), and develop staff interests and initiatives. (Deputy Education Officer)

> The X consortium has to be self-funding: there is a person in Indonesia drumming up students for a 10 per cent cut. (Educational Consultant)

> The market mechanism puts resources in the best place. In economically depressed areas, colleges can become centres of excellence for something: Y attracted foreign students. It is a question of finding markets. (Chamber of Commerce Officer)

Another, however, challenged the possibility of adopting a true market approach in the present system:

> If market forces were allowed to operate, we would have a decent system. What we have is a politically manipulated market. How else would you get government policy to work? The English system responds to industrial and government pressure for producing personnel for industries. On the Continent you find people training to earn a living, and you find market growth. In England, industrial needs are identified too late. We get short-term manpower planning and a reduction in employment as productivity methods displace people. We train for dying industries. Established industries have a hard lean on provision.

We're not responding to a group of people, but to political pressures. (CGLI Officer)

Nevertheless, despite such reservations, approximately one in six interviewees was prepared to make a case for and/or draw attention to the rewards of a commercial approach in CFEs, of which the following are examples:

I'd like to see the responsive college making money out of training by supplying to local firms. In the town of Z, the LEA said that CFEs could keep 90 per cent of the profit from courses responding to the needs of local firms. G College has a lower status, but when a major manufacturer came to Z, the college went to them and undercut the University of Z in bidding to provide computer courses. They got an advance payment from the manufacturer and set up their own unit in the college. (Chamber of Commerce Officer)

Where education is voluntary, marketing is vital. The skills and the tools are available. It is not sensible not to use communications and the media to create public awareness. (Industrial Training Officer)

I'm in favour of colleges selling expertise in order to generate income. It gives an opportunity for co-operation in the EEC where a UK company has a West German branch. (Conservative MP)

Selling expertise is in principle a good thing. CFEs have always tried to do consultancy if they have skills and knowledge. It would help them to keep up to date and in touch with reality. (Chamber of Commerce Officer)

I agree with the principle as with consultants in medicine who have free selling time. This has two advantages: skills are not lost to industry; it allows thinking time and updating and feedback. For CFEs at the moment, the only measure is the pass rate. (Industrial Trainer)

Should colleges generate income? In the present scenario that means YTS and adult retraining, as in PICKUP. On both scores the answer is yes. (DES Official)

Colleges need 'reserves' to be adaptable. (Educational Consultant)

Colleges should be skilled in maximising income from all sources. They should be 'funding programmes' not 'programming funds'. Rather than putting on programmes to attract funds, they should have programmes already and be looking for funds. (Senior LEA Adviser)

However, in spite of such endorsements as those provided above - and the last quotation might be seen as anti-marketing as well - the overwhelming majority of our respondents displayed at least ambivalence, and sometimes distrust, towards the commercial approach. Even some of the above respondents suggested reservations at other points in their interviews. The missionary and the marketeer appear to have irreconcilable attitudes. Co-existence is possible, but not always comfortable.

In part, the feeling of an uneasy alliance being formed between CFEs and the world of business must derive from current Government endeavours to enable colleges to become profit centres. In the past, the kinds of activities mentioned above (full-cost courses, lettings, etc.) have arisen on an *ad hoc* basis and have been left to the enterprise and commitment of individuals. Going 'public', as it were, putting pressure on all CFEs to generate income, tends to shift the emphasis from choice to necessity. As the effects of a reduced birth rate wreak their consequences upon CFEs, the more thrusting, innovative and responsive the college - the more commercially minded - the more likely it is to survive amidst competition. The unease is understandable.

Two of our respondents worked for LEAs which were seeking to control the market situation through local government policy:

We're setting target student numbers and funding on the basis of targets. Failure to achieve the target will result in redeployment of resources and a reduction of college budgets. It's not interventionist, but a strategy to let managers take initiatives. I hesitate to use the expression 'stick in the hand'. We're trying to remove shackles. If the college increases its numbers, it will get more resources. At the moment we're at a student intake peak. Later there will be a fight to get increasing shares of a diminishing market. (FE Inspector)

We had a training voucher system. The voucher was seen as a critical factor. The system was seen to be demand, not supply, led. It wasn't packing people into the supply side. (Assistant Education Officer)

Two respondents simply did not trust the LEA, whatever the merits of a marketing approach:

I've got to be sure that we don't suffer as a result. The LEA have given us permission to do this, but the money has to go through the LEA. (Head of Department)

If CFEs could be autonomous, it might lead to responsiveness, but it is more likely to be a cost-cutting exercise and therefore less responsive. (Education Consultant)

One respondent rejected the autonomous model:

People have mooted that colleges should be virtually independent entities and that the LEA should be responsible for what the college does not provide, either persuading the college to offer it, or going to somebody else. In the present state of affairs, that isn't a realistic way forward. (DES Official)

Another had doubts about how the CFE would survive in the market:

It makes sense for universities and polys who are closer to industry and the market and who have the more clever and learned people: they could be consultants. I'm not sure about CFEs. They should broaden their brief and ability to supply . . . maybe for low skills. (Employers Federation Officer)

The competitive ethic was questioned by others:

We need a body to help with markets and stop colleges competing unnecessarily with one another. Although I would want competition, there is some over-competition at the moment. (ITB Officer)

I don't know about CFEs as profit centres. It sounds totally destructive and short-sighted, like skill centres who won't touch the unskilled. The needs of the neglected and the needs of the country have to be met. (Labour MP)

The 'needs' issue rose from time to time: if CFEs adopt a business ethic, who will provide the non-profitable training? Part of the mythology of public sector provision is that it serves the interests of minority groups who would be neglected by the private sector because their demands or their numbers make such activities unprofitable. Privatise public transport, the argument runs, and the popular routes will be covered more cheaply and the less popular routes not at all. Commercialise the BBC and Pergolesi's concerti and Bolivian folk songs will disappear forever from the airwaves[1].

1. Although one might currently query whether BBC2 or the commercial Channel 4 caters more fully for minority tastes. On the other hand, some would argue that the existence of non-commercial broadcasting influences commercial broadcasting which might behave differently in a totally commercial market.

Of course, the issues/variables involved are both too complex and too many to allow for easy proof or accurate prediction. At the same time the notion of responsiveness to unprofitable minority needs does not square with the allegations of provider-centredness in colleges, unless, that is, the decision about which 'loss leaders' are to be offered is left to the whims/commitments of individual staff. Trying to formulate broad policy initiatives raises other problems, the questions of priority and range, the necessity for political support. Education/training to meet the needs of women, the unemployed, ethnic minorities have already been mentioned in quotations from some of our respondents: does one stop there? The 'disadvantaged' are an amorphous group whose claims can often seem to be in competition, particularly in a period of economic recession. How does one decide?

> I accept the need for 'social service' provision, but how far do you go? Where do you draw the line? Do you put on special courses for black lesbians? I don't know . . . marketing must establish real needs. (DES Official)

While our brief was to examine the extent to which CFEs were meeting the needs of industry/commerce, and not to attempt to establish a ranking order among different college client groups/market segments, nonetheless the existence of such demands continually impinged on responses to the questions we put. For one group of respondents, the commercial approach was not to be dismissed, but neither was it to be unreservedly welcomed. Caution seemed to obtrude:

> A consultancy role for colleges has potential, but it could be abused. It's a question of who benefits. (Industrial Training Officer)

> I'm not against 'selling expertise', but there has to be accountability and I would like to see the involvement of students, for example, in marketing. (SDP Spokesperson)

> I would support profit centres, but with safeguards, if it would help responsiveness. But you would have to watch out for commercial law which might mean that needs would not be met. (Voluntary Organisation Researcher)

> Most of them do it now. If there is a good dialogue, you don't need consultants. The question of who's charging whom could be detrimental to relationships. We have no objection, but if the educational standards dropped, we would worry. You would need control and spare activity or extra lecturers. (Training Deputy Head, Nationalised Industry)

> We said a guarded welcome as long as it doesn't divert attention and prevent the non-profit making activities. (TUC Officer)

However, it would be quite wrong to suggest that the reservations about adopting a more commercial approach to college management are centred solely (or even primarily) on the question of which client groups are to be served, with potentially profitable/loss-making results. There is the matter of selling/promotion/advertising, hawking or hustling: how does this fit into the world of the CFE? To some extent it is already present, but not sufficiently so for some CFE onlookers. The Audit Commission (1985) recommends

Promotion of college services through membership of chambers of trade and commerce, direct contact with overseas government agencies, advertising in the local press and council newsheets, and through use of libraries, careers advisory centres, Job Centres and other public offices to display available courses and facilities.

Davies and Scribbins (1985) suggest that

... effective promotion is an essential element in ensuring that the services provided by a college are taken up by the full range of people who can benefit from them.

and then go on to offer advice on writing to persuade, advertising in newspapers, magazines, journals, local radio and cinema, establishing a corporate image, direct mailing, personal promotion, the utilisation of promotional events (exhibitions, open days and conferences) organising a sales interview, relations with the media, writing press releases, conducting radio and TV interviews, etc. The tone is cautious, and prospective converts are assured that

No deception or overblown promises need be involved: simply a commitment to understanding the viewpoint of the potential customers and presenting the information in the manner which they can appreciate best.

Yet between no advertising, or an uninspiring prospectus, on the one hand and 'deception' and 'overblown promises' on the other, there is a great deal of middle ground which might, for some colleges, represent an area for exploration. Should college advertising exploit the insecurities of prospective clients, their competititiveness or concupiscence? What of visually subliminal advertising where, through association, products are 'sold' with images of affluence or sexual desirability? Some of our competitors had grave doubts:

I'm suspicious of advertising. (DES Official)

Others raised the question of going 'the whole way':

Retailing staff need social skills. In California they receive in-service training .. how to smile, what to say. Perhaps we are too sophisticated in the UK, too learned . . . Perhaps we ought to go to drama classes to learn how to smile. (Director of Education)

If one can detect a note of irony, the disbelieving rhetorically confronting the insupportable, others were less reticent and spoke out for the advantages of effective 'packaging':

> CFEs need to employ communications and the media to create public awareness. We are full of hype: the first thirty feet of a store is clear and tidy, but backstage . . . (Personnel Manager, large food chain)

> There is a need for FE to sell itself better: people don't like bare classrooms. They like carpeted rooms. Part of responsiveness is meeting current standards of comfort. (HMI)

> If you train YTS trainees in the college's reception area, you won't get company directors coming to the college. (Assistant Education Officer)

Moreover, selling is not solely the business of informing people of what they 'need', however one defines it, but also of creating a demand for what they palpably do not need. What of 'repackaging', getting rid of surplus stocks, in college terms flogging underemployed lecturers to teach undersubscribed courses, possibly a 'sale' or a 'special'?

> It's worth a try. I suspect most colleges will have a helluva job. A fifty-year old mechanical engineering lecturer with a clapped-out workshop is hard to repackage. (DES Official)

There is also the question of profits, and who gets them. At present LEAs vary as to the extent to which they 'claw back' college earnings, some allowing virtually none and others practically all of the profits to accrue to the college. And if to the college, precisely to whom in the college? Our respondents encompassed a varied range of attitudes:

> Colleges have to be cost centres. They shouldn't have to go to the LEA for trivial funds. The profit should go to the college, not to lecturers or the LEA. The college mustn't have an unfair advantage in competition with other consultants. (Industrial Trainer)

the last sentence offering an interesting perception, and a recognition that from a commercial point of view colleges can seem excessively well placed competitively. From the inside, of course, things might look somewhat different and the spotlight might be focused elsewhere:

> I would support, and have operated, profits for both the college and individual benefits. As far as the college is concerned, you have to be clear about who is getting the profit: it could be a

department, or even a section of a department, that might benefit. (MSC Officer, ex-principal)

Another principal, who considered that lecturers were 'paid well' and who had last year cut out £200,000 of contracted overtime for staff, was altogether less certain about whether staff should benefit personally:

Separate contract work is liked by all, but it needs turning round. It needs to be approached in a structured way. It needs to benefit the city and the employers before it benefits individuals.

At the DES, a civil servant saw the need for 'turning round' from the other side: with regard to whether staff should be allowed to earn a 'commission' from generated income he suggested that he

. . . would go quite a long way in that direction. I might have to draw in my claws if things went wrong, but the pendulum is now so far in the other direction . . . a swing of the pendulum is needed. There should be rewards for people who go out and innovate. A reward structure is needed . . . a conscious policy to reward innovation, not just degree work.

while a colleague on another floor of Elizabeth House was less certain:

Whether staff should be allowed to keep commissions . . . it's an interesting idea . . . why not? . . . Some people might take a different line[2].

Overtime contracts have for long been a means by which staff in CFEs have been induced either to take on additional work (whether above their notional maximum) or to support innovative initiatives. The underlying issue is one of motivitation: how can one persuade the individual to expend additional effort? **Report of policy group** (MSC/LAA, 1985) offers some fairly traditional answers:

The main incentives for the college related to the extra income derived from full cost courses and the enhancement of their image in the community. The staff were felt to be motivated by their professional commitment. In some cases direct links with industry enhanced their ability to gain from consultancy work and secondment to industry improved career prospects and job security were also mentioned as incentives.

where we can detect the familiar blend of the missionary ('professional commitment') and the marketeer ('gain from consultancy work')

2. Among those who 'might' one would expect to find the Audit Commission (1985) who would clearly wish to limit the payment of overtime to those already working their full contracted hours: 'Not infrequently, full-time lecturers are found to be working overtime or to have part-time teaching contracts as their own college whilst falling far short of providing their full-time hours'.

approaches.

A similar mixture could be detected among our respondents:

> You can't facilitate motivation. It is self generated. A personal crisis may induce people to act, but human nature is such that not everyone would act. (Industrial Training Officer)

> The College will not be responsive unless the people who put in the work are seen to be rewarded, whether by a study tour to the West Coast or by being given preference when vacancies arise[3]. (DES Official)

Such mixed motives as those outlined above can be found not only among colleges as providers, but also among their clients. Two such individuals made clear that their own college support was founded on personal convenience:

> I'm not impressed by fly-by-night companies. I prefer to use the college. I have more faith in the public sector because of their professional base. We could do some courses ourselves, but we use the college because we can turn the tap on and off. They find this painful, but they do it. We are aware of this. (Training Officer, Nationalised Industry)

> The cut, cloth and quality of the suit is defined by the customer. This is hard to take at lecturer level . . . We want to continue using colleges because they have hardware worth about £50,000,000. It would be absurd not to use them. (ITB Training Officer)

If one looks over the above quotations, what emerges is an underlying sense of ambiguity, the missionary/marketeer roles uncertainly coupled. This is true collectively among our respondents, but also - even if less apparently so without complete interview transcripts - for individuals as well. As noted, the marketeer tradition is well established in universities, and even considerably evident in CFEs, although with the 'profit motive' somewhat disguised. The explanation lies largely in the autonomy of universities, sometimes referred to (despite funding from public money) as the 'private sector', as contrasted with the 'local' college which is legally the

---

3. We ought to distinguish perhaps between *motivation* (OED: to motivate, 'to furnish with a motive') and *commitment*. While the latter may be 'self generated', the former, frequently involving short-term acquiescence, is often within the grasp of most managers: flattery, pressure and money, even small amounts, seem to work frequently in education. Of course, it is unlikely that any manager can motivate everyone in the organisation, or anyone on every occasion, but it is unlikely that either will be necessary. Even in commercial firms, for example, some salesmen will bring in less business than others, may live quite happily with their levels of achievement, and many even be encouraged/permitted to do so, provided they do not fall below an acceptable norm. Commitment, however, is often advanced as the prerogative of the professional. One suspects that, like most things in life, it waxes and wanes throughout a career, if it may be said to have existed in the first place.

'child' of the LEA, which, in at least some instances, takes nearly full charge of the CFE's earnings. However, it would be insufficient to suggest that legal status alone accounts for the currently uncertain reaction of CFEs to the promotion and advocacy of extended business approaches. We need also to point to the other sources of incipient tension:

1. **Education/training as a storage device.** For many years, technological development, and more recently unemployment, have led to the utilisation of education/training as a repository for individuals in order to shorten the labour market. This has been justified on the grounds of both necessity and, perhaps less openly so, expediency. In the traditionally elitist British system, filtering people through from infant school to university, the retention of greater numbers of people in the system for longer and longer periods has made the traditional offerings inappropriate for those who would previously have been filtered out. The MSC 'takeover' of at least a part of school and college provision may be seen as grounded in the conviction that teachers/lecturers were unwilling, or unable, to extend their range of offerings and to accommodate a largely new clientele without external pressure. It is difficult to avoid acknowledging that this movement, closely linked to the new commercial/marketing approach, has generated at least a part of the resulting animosity/ambivalence. Colleges have been made to confront new students, new offerings, new methods, new competences, the New FE, and not always with enthusiasm. CFEs are being forced to move down market and to cater for more demanding market segments.

2. **The reward system.** The New FE has made new and difficult demands, accompanied by widespread resourcing cuts, or so some have alleged. With the growth of marketing approaches, and MSC revenue, especially in pre-YTS days, the more enterprising principals/colleges have been able to offset losses in one direction with gains in others, particularly if they have worked within supportive authorities. The real scale of inflicted wounds from resourcing cuts in CFEs has probably been less extensive than in some other kinds of educational establishments. Shouting is a useful defensive strategy often intended to discourage would-be attackers, so it remains difficult to gauge the real damage done. In interview, one principal acknowledged:

> Cuts? I'm tempted to say, 'What cuts?' The number of staff has never been reduced, although posts have been frozen. The authority offers three years' enhancement for premature retirement, but few take it. All redundancies have been voluntary. The cuts have been largely in finance, capital and revenue. A cut back? No. A stand still? Yes.

Whatever the familiarity or otherwise of the above experience, from an individual lecturer's point of view the most personally damaging cuts are deeply embedded in the reward system. In public-sector FHE, the categorisation of work and the attachment of a greater proportion of posts above Lecturer I to the higher categories of work means that moving down market entails the likelihood not merely of harder work and the development of new skills, but also of reduced pay and promotion prospects. The central irony of the Audit Commission (1985) report lies not in its exhortations to LEAs to make lecturers increase their efficiency and productivity (larger classes taught less frequently, less 'over-grading of staff', etc.), but that it does so, at least in part, with the expectation of promulgating a more commercial approach to college activity. Lecturers are thus chided for being ineffective marketeers (a 'failure to assess and exploit the market') and missionaries ('lost opportunities for potential students') simultaneously.

3. **Institutional politics.** One may argue that what the CNAA has been to colleges of education, the MSC is currently to CFEs, albeit while playing a somewhat different role and employing rather different strategies. Nonetheless, both have undertaken as part of their mission the designation of courses and skills (and, hence, staff) as at least partially redundant from the point of view of client needs. As it works its way through the establishment, such a realisation has the effect of undermining the institutional hierarchy, both at the level of formal organisation and among private individuals. The market-place knows both sudden fortunes and unexpected crashes, and it offers no refuge for the latter. Some university departments may be able to convince their pay-masters that 'centres of excellence' in Old Icelandic poetry and Egyptian archaeology represent 'special cases' for protection, but in the rougher world of the CFE, it is likely to become increasingly difficult to escape market forces. Old stars will fall and new ones rise. Pecking orders will be reformed.

4. **The environment.** The effects of a decline in the birth rate are due to work their way through FE and into HE in the next few years. The result will be not merely competition within the college, but also among and between colleges and other institutions. Despite (or perhaps because of) open/distance learning, the likelihood is that we shall soon have too many institutions to support existing traditional education/training demands: the fight for survival will commence. An awareness of the difficulties probably exists somewhere below the surface, but at present, and during the past few years, CFEs have been struggling to feed through the last population 'bulge', for which reason the impending market decline may have been easy to ignore. However, the kinds of contraction pains experienced by colleges of education and many schools will ultimately reach post-compulsory education. The marketing approach is therefore the harbinger for many colleges of a necessary opening up of new markets, with the need to acknowledge a product's life cycle and to promote a constantly evolving

market mix (Davies and Scribbens, 1985). College staff will have to work harder to survive in an increasingly turbulent environment.

That the current advocacy of a commercial/marketing approach to education/training should be met with ambivalence is hardly surprising. It represents not a new departure for CFEs, but an enforced personal and political realignment along the missionary-marketeer continuum, an attempt to shift colleges firmly towards the latter. That shift occurred many generations ago in the United States, from a scrutiny of whose system many of the **Competence and competition** recommendations derive, but in Britain the prospect of a similar shift promoted conspicuously and openly, where marketing was once undertaken discreetly and privately, arouses unease. The majority of our respondents may be said to have supported the market approach, but with reservations. Even so, it is impossible to assert that their support was not partly engendered by the nature of our task, an enquiry into CFE responsiveness to industry/commerce. Their reservations, on the other hand, are deeply rooted in tradition and in the missionary ideal. What is fairly apparent is that few of our respondents had at the time of their interviews thought through the likely consequences of an increasing commitment in education/training to marketeering, or identified the likely issues. Their evidence suggests tentative exploration of uncharted territory. Caution abounds.

Yet, it is highly improbable that the shift to a more commercial approach in CFEs can be stopped or even curtailed, or that its origins lie purely in the advocacy of the present Government and its agencies. Powerful environmental forces - major demographic movements accompanied by rapidly accelerating technological change - leave education/training with no option but to respond increasingly sensitively to client needs in the interests of survival. Marketing is essentially a metaphor being adopted by a service industry whose traditional services/products are rapidly coming to be offered in an ex-seller's market which is progressively becoming a buyer's market. Marketing is thus an acknowledgement of a shift of power, from provider to client.

Summary

In recent years, CFEs have come under mounting pressure to adopt a more 'businesslike' approach to their affairs, to concern themselves with generating at least (but an increasing) part of their income, with operating more efficiently, and with adopting a marketing perspective. While the exhortations have frequently sought changes in kind, the more likely modifications are in the direction of degree, since many colleges have for some time been at least partially committed to a business model. However, there remain many unresolved tensions centred on the missionary-marketeer dichotomy: how does one reconcile minority needs with profitability? selling with serving? manipulating the market with meeting needs? How does one distribute college profits? Confronted with such dilemmas, our respondents displayed considerable ambivalence and some distrust of the advocated approaches, offering little in the direction of possible resolution, while understandably aware of the potential disadvantages.

Such anxieties, it was argued, need to be viewed within the larger context of major changes currently assailing CFEs: an increasing use of education/training to reduce unemployment numbers, with a resultant 'down-market' shift in CFE work; an inherited reward system which penalises just such a shift; consequent destabilising of internal college political structures; and impending competition for a declining market where CFEs will have to compete with both schools and HE institutions, the harbinger of a dramatic movement from a seller's to a buyer's market, of the increasing subordination of provider to client needs.

Chapter 7

MARKET RESEARCH: MANAGEMENT THROUGH INPUT CONTROLS

In terms of a systems/product cycle model (discussed in Appendix B), most current exhortations to enhanced CFE effectiveness tend to concentrate on better quality input in general and on market research in particular. **Competence and competition** (NEDC/MSC, 1984) urges colleges to

> ... go to their potential customers with the offer of providing for their needs and wishes ...

The Audit Commission (1985) suggests that

> Marketing covers both the assesment of short-term and long-term need and the 'selling' of education and training opportunities to students and prospective employers.

The interim CELP report (DES, 1985) identifies in its list of conclusions

> ... the need for colleges to go to employers to ascertain their precise needs, and then to react flexibly and quickly to them.

The MSC/LAA (1985) **Report of policy group** sets out its recommendations for Local Development Plans and draws its attention to the value of

> ... improving the information base and developing marketing systems ...

The **MSC/LAA guidance handbook** (1985) to the above emphasises the importance of

> ... extended opportunities for consultation with other employers and other bodies.

College employer links are obviously a cause for concern.

We might begin by asking what has been the nature of those links prior to the present 'concern'. In **Education for employees** (1984), HMI reported that 77 per cent of the colleges in their survey had good or adequate links with employers, although only a few months later, following the publication of the **Training for jobs** White Paper (DE/DES, 1984), the **CELP 3 Bulletin** (DES 1984) had occasion to record ruefully that

> ... HMI found that college-employer links were adequate or better in only three quarters of the colleges visited ...

One might well question whether in a world in which nothing is a 100 per cent 'three quarters' should attract the adverb 'only'.

Traditionally, CFE market research in recent years has centred on the advisory committee, 'formal links between college departments and local employers' (DES, 1985) where representatives of both sides meet in general once per term. The CELP interim report (DES, 1985) lists five drawbacks to such arrangements:

> ... poor attendance by employer's representatives ... uncertainty about the role of the committees ... college dominated discussion ... a pre-occupation with past achievements ... little involvement by the committees in policy, planning and marketing ...

These points were corroborated by many of our respondents:

> I don't want advisory committees. They're an expensive waste of time. I'm looking for relationships between heads and principals and representatives of industry. I want fewer more highly powered committees. In advisory committees, you get heads going on for two hours about how good their departments are. (Principal)

> Maybe we send the wrong people to advisory groups, or we can't get them 'clued up'. (Employers Federation Officer)

> We need to make sure that advisory committee representatives are up to date. At every college you get opinions coming from men twenty years out of date. They don't know the names, never mind the aims. They have a capacity for stopping new things. (ITB Officer)

> I visit about four colleges a week. All of them have advisory committees. Few of them are effective in my experience. More progressive colleges have disbanded or reorganised in a special way. Heads are appointing people to deal with specific firms. It's much more precise. In some subjects you get a huge spread of conflicting interests among committee members and the committee becomes a matter of a cup of coffee three times a year. This is beginning to disappear. Of course some committees do work . . . (BTEC Regional Coordinator)

> Advisory committees might be useful, but they're not of much use with pretty significant staffing problems. They're too open, formal and public. In practice advisory committees are of limited use, and by and large not worth the effort. I have a lot of time for ad hoc groupings of various interests concerned who are asked and required to report on something specific by an agreed date. (MSC officer)

We made a requirement,which didn't exist before, that industry must be involved in formulating and preparing programmes, and it's an ongoing requirement. We are dealing with 500 colleges, the whole spectrum. It,s difficult to see how meaningful it is. X is the *raison d'etre,* but in other colleges committees meet once a term, paying lip-service. Most colleges probably had consultative committees, but we've given it a higher profile. (BTEC Officer)

The MSC/LAA **Report** (1985) expands on the above:

BTEC felt that the existence of formal local consultative machinery was no guarantee of effective links between colleges and employers and that better links were forged where their successful operation was recognised by according recognition and status to the individuals in the college involved.

In contrast and isolation, one must report the principal respondent who claimed otherwise:

We're responsive through college committees. We have an active academic board and sub-committees. Technically they're advisory, but I have to have a good reason for not accepting their advice.

and the Deputy Education Officer who wanted to try again:

Consultative committees should be made to work.

Pace the above quotations, the clear impression from both the literature and our respondents is that the advisory committees (or indeed committees[1] in general) do not/cannot work as a market research tool, whatever other purposes they may serve. Indeed to the CELP list of limitations quoted above we ought also to add inadequate and inappropriate employer representation.

A group of respondents developed the point made by the BTEC Coordinator above, that specific contacts (often on a one-to-one basis) for specific purposes are most useful:

The last thing to do is to have a meeting. People should go out and meet one another on a one-to-one basis. We should introduce college people one by one in industry, get people to use college facilities. You have to build up relationships over time. I've seen it happen well in France where local industry is involved with the college because of a one per cent apprenticeship tax and a one per cent training tax. The employer can spend it where he likes at

1. MSC/LAA (1985) report that 'The number of industrial representatives can vary from 5-10 out of the total membership (which also varied between 26-30 members)' of governing bodies.

recognised centres. If he has receipts, he is released from tax liability. (ITB Officer)

Lower down you need a marketing person at L2 to market the college courses. This is happening more and more. It focuses interest and upsets hierarchy and territory. (Industrial Trainer)[2]

However, whatever the arrangement for bringing employers and college staff together to determine the requirements of the former, the next consideration is what and how they are to do whatever it is they are supposed to do. Davis and Scribbins (1985) take the grand view, albeit somewhat cautiously, providing a caveat about duplicated effort among colleges/LEAs, but noting the desirability of

. . . Basic demographic information: the profile of potential customers in terms of age, sex, income groups, occupations and social status . . . The geographical distribution of potential customers: a local or national map of relevant population density can be constructed . . . The nature of distributive channels, e.g. road, bus and train networks to the college . . .

Such information might well be useful, but its appearance without (or even with) the establishment of marketing units in each college or LEA seems problematical. The MSC/LAA (1985) **Report** notes of the present scene:

There is on the evidence submitted, little input at present from the MSC of manpower forecasts and training needs. Although there are employer and other inputs to decisions about national (now to be reviewed) qualifications on offer locally and both formal and, perhaps better, informal discussions at local level, the local inputs are often to be described as 'individual' rather than that of local employers as a whole.

One of our respondents suggested that such information was unlikley to be forthcoming:

The MSC haven't got local labour market information at the moment, and I have grave doubts about its materialising. In terms of numbers and operational statistics, I don't think they will provide it. (MSC Officer)

One may therefore question the practicality of expecting small local colleges (or even LEAs) to acquire market data of the kind available to multi-

---

2. The CFE concern with internal hierarchy is somewhat amusingly if unintentionally revealed in the **Responsibility and responsiveness** (Kedney/Parkes, 1985) case study where the writer identifies a course development team membership in terms of 'a lecturer grade II, a senior lecturer and head of department' and 'representatives' from five companies.

and international enterprises. Moreover, there will always remain the difference between the college with a geographically small catchment area in a region of high population density with a small number of large employers, and the institution drawing its students from a wide circumference and surrounded by (literally) hundreds of employers. The point is that one cannot reasonably anticipate miracles with the limited resources available, despite the Audit Commission's query (1985) about whether a more careful utilisation of remission might not make time available 'for research and marketing'. One suspects that in many colleges 'grand' holistic market research is likely to be hit and miss, ad hoc and un-coordinated, if only because the projected task is too great for the means available.

At the same time, attempts to gather more mundane data are also likely to encounter difficulties. Even if the college moves towards a system of personal contacts with individual employers, it is still necessary to ask what it is the researcher wants to know, and how he will recognise it when it surfaces. Using the definitions established above for primary clients (students) and secondary clients (all the rest, including employers), we may expect the college to need to distinguish between:

1. **felt needs,** identified by primary/secondary clients (students, employers wishing to buy in skills) and directed at the college system in terms of demands/wants, i.e. education/training which is actively sought, and

2. **perceived needs,** in the sense of deficiencies noted by (would-be?) agents/secondary clients as observable in current/potential students/ primary clients.

We come yet again to, to the missionary-marketeer dichotomy, to the possible difference between what secondary clients paternalistically believe is good for primary clients and/or other secondary clients and what the latter two groups may actually wish, i.e. to the needs/wants issue:

In a number of instances, where the issue seemed to arise in response to other questions, we additionally asked respondents if there was a distinction between needs and wants. One sidestepped the issue:

> I don't distinguish. There's no point. Needs are provided by public activity (resourced) to satisfy identified need. Of course the identifiers of need are difficult to identify. With the private desires of individuals, many can be fitted into the curriculum. Sometimes they pay for them personally. City and Guilds meet the identified needs of industry. (CGLI Officer)

Another approached differentiation without any pretence of refinement:

> In some cases it's comparatively easy. You have records of individual companies. In other cases, it's by guess and by God. (Principal)

Two respondents suggested that colleges should attempt to persuade clients to remedy deficiencies:

> What is a need? Expressed demand is not always a real need. A responsive college is a college with coherent and continued thinking about how need should be interpreted and not in traditional or fanciful ways . . . It's easier to respond to employers when there is a close link, not a dialogue, but the CFE does what it is asked. A more sensitive college will argue that the company should be doing more. (Educational Consultant)

> If you have to, you can distinguish by looking at the constituency of employers. That should separate them out. It doesn't tell you what to go for. The responsive college will be turning round to various constituencies and saying, 'Your preparation of needs is inadequate . . .'(MSC Officer)

Another sought to close the potential gap by an emphasis on facilitation:

> A CFE should meet all the expressed needs of industry and commerce and should be in a position to help industry and commerce to determine training needs. (LEA Senior Adviser)

but two others advanced the primacy of wants above all else:

> I tell CFEs what I want, but don't get it. (Chamber of Commerce Officer)

> If industry makes a request, the principal shouldn't query industry's intelligence. It's not for the principal to decide what is appropriate provision. (Industrial Trainer)

Regardless of any such difficulties, a group of our repondents had no doubt of the value of undertaking market research:

> We're trying to identify resources to support marketing research through a specific post in each college. We're hoping to develop eight to ten county subject boards, with heads of subject in the colleges, MSC, employers. (FE Inspector)

> I know a number of colleges where lecturers tend to say, 'I'm always here. My door is open'. In more successful colleges, lecturers go out. I knew one head who went out on his bike during September into industry. (ITB Officer)

> Only employers can assess their training needs, i.e. discern the broad type of training needs and quality of people. But they can't identify the FE content because they are too busy producing. However, they can advise regarding trends in industry and the technological changes. (Employers Federation Officer)

Although the MSC/LAA (1985) **Report** concludes that 'few colleges had a formal system for collecting data', at least one respondent suggested that requisite work might be going on elsewhere:

> We did a survey of more than one thousand companies, using face-to-face interviews. We asked what they did, what happens, not opinions, not people saying what they think. We then asked City and Guilds to review the syllabuses in the light of our findings. (ITB Officer)

However, there exists in the literature, and among some of our respondents, the conviction that real market research is difficult (or even impossible) to carry out successfully. The HMI (1985) study of part-time TEC Higher Certificate Programmes in Engineering notes that

> ...it proved extremely difficult to get the employers to be specific and analytical about the contribution the FE college programme was expected to make . . . It was even more difficult to get employers to assess the over-all achievement of college programmes.

Bradshaw (1984) advances a similar conclusion:

> The assumption is also made throughout the White Paper that industry is clear in the knowledge of what it wants. The experience of many colleges is that though some industries can, many cannot say what they want in the way of training.

The CELP (DES, 1985) interim report lists among its conclusions

> . . . the need for employers to formulate their needs precisely and to understand the other demands, and the constraints on colleges.

The existence of the species, 'the inarticulate industrialist', is affirmed by several of our respondents.

> The whole responsive business is a cop out after years of neglect. The dimension of responsiveness takes on a twist with respect to competitiveness of UK Ltd. In that context colleges can't be very much more responsive than the quality of requests, the articulation of requests, they receive from industry. (FEU Officer)

> Industry gets its messages scrambled. We don't know what they want. They don't either. CBI and Rolls Royce may know, but they don't represent the majority. (HMI)

> There's a belief that employers are not good at articulating what they want. (MSC Officer)

75

We are back again with the unreasonableness of employers, a characteristic corroborated by a representative from their own ranks:

> Training officers in companies are also reactive. They complain about CFEs but wait for the booklets to arrive on their desks. (Industrial Training Development Officer)

Retaliatory complaints appear in the two reports prepared for Birmingham LEA by a commercial market research organisation (TACIT, 1985) and in the CELP interim report (DES, 1985)

> As the consultants to one area reported 'The colleges are regarded as a typical state run monopoly and most users feel that they have not bothered to market themselves more positively because they have felt secure in the knowledge that no one would challenge their position. This image and perception has led to the view by industry that colleges are not worth approaching for any new or out of the ordinary courses except for YTS.' Common criticisms were of: the quality of college reporting on student/training progress . . . confusing information . . . inflexible timetabling . . . excessive institutional independence leading to duplication of some provision but gaps in other places . . . the poor impression given to visitors and telephone callers . . . Many employers, rightly or wrongly, believe college staff to be out of date and unfamiliar with modern industrial and commercial operations . . .

In response to which we can find the ball thrown firmly back:

> The difficulty is that you can write to the SATROs and the CBIs etc. and get predictable responses, but an empirical study of individual small employers would show different characteristics because small employers are not represented on the CBI. There is also the question of scale. If you look at an LEA you could find influential small employers expressing clearly defined needs, but does this relate to the CBI view? (Voluntary Organisation Researcher)

and back again:

> There's the economic issue of two colleges fighting and marketing for the same product. (Industrial Trainer)

and yet again in the MSC/LAA (1985) **Report**:

> Industry liaison with colleges was felt to be inadequate, it was rare for employers regularly to consult with the colleges. They needed to be more articulate in identifying and planning their needs, although many colleges accepted that employers did not always

know what they wanted and the colleges had a useful role to play in offering support to industry in identifying its needs.

and back to where we started via the CELP (1985) interim report:

> The pilot projects have reported that while employers show interest in further education when approached, they seldom take the initiative to approach colleges themselves to set down their training needs. This may in part reflect other calls on their time (especially in the case of small businesses) but it may also reflect industry's poor view of the further education system.

Charge and counter-charge, criticism and complaint: where does one break the circle? The CELP report quoted from above reaches its conclusions with an attitude of majesterial even-handedness, passing three 'problems' to employers and three to colleges. It is a comfortable onlooker's position, easy to defend, if necessary, but also firmly outside the combat arena.

In part the problem arises from the attitudes of CFEs. Just as teachers tend to prefer commited/compliant students with a love of learning, so they seem to exhibit a predeliction for clients/customers with a talent for delineating their needs precisely and clearly. In the world of the market-place, however, there is no necessity for customers to be articulate, reasonable, consistent, or even particularly rational. Customers often do not know what they want, or even change their minds and try to return goods. Customers can also be unpleasant and disagreeable, bad tempered and sharp tongued. The maxim tells us that 'the customer is always right', and the language also preserves a range of epithets in which 'customer' is qualified by a pithy adjective to indicate an unpleasant individual: *a tough customer, an ugly customer, a rum customer*. It is at the point at which CFEs complain about their customers that the colleges appear most provider-centred, least client-centred. Moreover, as the enterprise moves down market, the customers tend to get rougher, the work harder, the profits smaller, and the volume of requisite sales correspondingly greater. The implications which lie beneath the aphorism 'market research' represent a major shift in organisational mission: in a buyer's market, the seller is very much more at the beck and call of the customer. The expectation is not merely that colleges will do the old things in new ways, but that they will be doing an increasing number of new things. To the extent that CFEs as a service industry become client-centred, the notion of a course or **the** course becomes meaningless, since what is offered must be modified for individuals and over time. Because individuals change, and indeed ought to do so as a consequence of their education/training, the necessity of identifying needs before the commencement of a course/programme diminishes. Similarly for employers, whose commercial worlds can suddenly make earlier assumptions and expectations suddenly invalid, as market costs/demands change.

However, the CFE desire to identify needs/wants prior to the student's arrival must be seen as part of a larger context. In terms of the systems model (Cf. Appendix B), British education can be characterised as provision which is controlled (or not, as some would argue) primarily through inputs. The sixties comprehensivisation movement was effected through efforts to alter intake into secondary schools, and into their classrooms by promoting mixed-ability grouping. The one undisputed area of DES control has for many years been in fixing teacher training numbers, and hence professional intake. A whole string of agencies exist to sanction courses as inputs, either through addition or limitation: RSA, CSE, GCE, CGLI, BTEC, RACs, CNAA, NAB, ACSET, etc. The assumption is that what comes out of the system is determined solely or primarily by what goes into it: if you want to change the system, change the inputs. Create a new examination, or rationalise existing examinations; or both. Alter syllabi. Undertake market research so as to feed new information/courses/programmes into the system[3].

It is hardly surprising that MSC should therefore seek to impact on the system by taking control of one of its major inputs, money. Indeed the MSC/LAA battle which raged throughout much of 1984 and 1985 appears to have ended in compromise through agreement on a new input, the local development plan, which the reconciled partners will now both be able to influence. In examining the discussion papers, what one notices is a detailed emphasis on calculations for inputs from the partners:

> It was agreed that the latest available FESR returns would be a prime consideration in determining allocations. (MSC/LAA, 1985)

> Figures on enrolments over previous years should be provided and some indication of support from employers for particular courses and areas of study; but equally future demand should be anticipated . . . (MSC, 1985)

In other words, future inputs would be based fundamentally on a consideration of previous inputs.

As I shall argue in subsequent chapters, the difficulty is that the system has very little activity which could be described as systematic and organised throughput monitoring. At the output/outcome end, there is some possible retrospective scrutiny of the throughput process via examinations and external monitoring, but there is no general consensus of what the analysis means, if anything. There is no agreement about performance indicators and output measures. It is, therefore, a system doomed to proceeding by a

3. A burgeoning business. There are eight CELP projects currently in operation and (at my last count) 12 major and 100 small-scale Local Collaborative Projects. The emphasis is on identifying needs and deciding 'how best to tackle them' (DES press notice, 1984) i.e. on inputs. The MSC/LAA (1985) **Report** records: 'The projects have concentrated initially on collecting employment and course data, seeking views about the effectiveness of local links and use made of colleges, and selecting topics for detailed examination'.

seemingly endless sequence of new initiatives, each destined to be judged (although through assertion rather than evidence) as eventually unsatisfactory and to be replaced by another initiative. The story of British education in recent years has to be written largely in terms of inputs, each promising outcomes which the system will make no structured and organised attempt to measure.

Summary

In British education/training, most efforts to alter CFE activity have concentrated on modifying inputs, with little organised effort directed at monitoring delivery and outcomes. Current advocacy of increased market research can be viewed as an attempt to acquire better information about what is needed/desired so as to modify course inputs. There are, however, a number of attendant difficulties. 1) Market research is problematical. There is uncertainty about the availability of accurate and useful information relating to middle/long-term local manpower needs, and whether such data can and will be provided, and by whom. 2) Traditionally, colleges have used advisory committees for information gathering, but our respondents tended to corroborate the view that such committees (whatever other purposes they may serve) do not function satisfactorily as data collection agencies, since they are considered frequently too large, public and unrepresentative. 3) Market research based on a one-to-one lecturer-employer contact already exists to some extent, but to increase the use of such an approach would be expensive, and precisely how and by whom it might be paid for has not been clearly established. 4) Attempts to modify college provision by establishing need prior to delivery assumes that clients can identify such needs exactly and that those needs will not be modified during the delivery process, neither of which may be necessarily true.

Chapter 8

THROUGHPUT MONITORING: HOW DO YOU IDENTIFY QUALITY?

Having spent so much time discussing responsiveness, it seemed reasonable that we should enquire of our respondents how they were able to determine its presence/absence. We consequently put two questions to them, again intended to view the problem from slightly different perspectives. Each question was often followed by a pause for thought or the admission that 'That's a hard one'. The first question (What criteria do you use to decide whether a college is responsive?) elicited 47 variables, one identified 17 times, but 28 offered once only. The results were as follows, with the number of respondents per variable in brackets when it was two or more:

1. **System inputs.** Approximately 40 per cent of our respondents identified criteria which might be described as reflecting CFE intention but which would not necessarily have to be accompanied by effective delivery.

a) **Marketing.** These were criteria centred on either a college search for client information and/or client access to college staff: marketing (2), market research, consultative committees (2), liaison with employers (17), number of open days, liaison with schools, other colleges and staff.

b) **Client groups:** actual demand (8), the ability to meet special needs with reference to gender and ethnic balance, the presence of non-traditional courses, new courses (9), and access.

c) **The syllabus:** course design (2), the amount of work experience involved, and assessment techniques.

2. **System throughput.** More than 46 per cent of our sample offered criteria which related to the throughput experience:

a) **Delivery.** Three respondents were literally concerned with aspects of delivery; when (opening hours), where (outreach courses), and how fast (speed). Others pointed to student perceptions of the learning experience: staff alertness, openness, flexibility (2), professionalism, adaptability (2), attitudes (2), and liveliness ('You can smell it'); but also classroom discipline, standards and quality, use of external lecturers; and student enjoyment and attendance/completion rates (6).

b) **College management.** Some respondents identified performance indicators in internal college activity on the part of staff: management structure, the pastoral system, staff development (4), the use of resources to meet needs (2), and evaluation techniques of the quality of teaching.

3. System output/outcomes. Nearly 43 per cent of respondents identified end-of-process criteria from the point of view of

a) **college staff:** profit, views of college staff;

b) **clients:** job take-up (7), examination results (6), whether the college had achieved client objectives (3), means for students to air views, informal feedback (5), reputation, testimonials from satisfied customers, follow up in the workplace (2), industrial (3) and student satisfaction, satisfaction with the fee in terms of value for money.

4. Input-outcome relationship. One respondent looked to what was said in committees and what actually happened.

Of our sample, 10 (19 per cent) offered no criteria for identifying college responsiveness. Of the remaining 44, 9 (20 per cent) suggested only input variables, 4 (9 per cent) only throughout, and 8 (18 per cent) only output; 4 (9 per cent) offered input and output variables, 3 (7 per cent) throughput and output, 8 (18 per cent) input and throughput, but of these fifteen only one saw an explicit relationship between one part of the process and another; 8 individuals (18 per cent) provided input, throughput and output criteria. The spread, and the extraordinarily varied range of ways in which respondents identified (or didn't) criteria, is perhaps reflective of the general lack of consensus over performance indicators and output measures. Some of the criteria (e.g. alertness, openness, flexibility, adaptability, liveliness) would appear to be beyond measurement in the current state of human development, so that one is reminded of the conclusion reached (Morgan *et al*, 1983) in the study of secondary school headteacher selection that both candidates and selectors were

> . . . forced to rely on 'hunch' and 'feel' rather than hard evidence.

There is very little hard evidence in the system.

Our second question (How can a college prove its responsiveness?) was meant to force respondents to scrutinise their own criteria as evidence, since intuitive judgements are not easily demonstrable of proof. One respondent would not play:

> Why should the college have to prove anything? (FEU Officer)

Several felt that proof was difficult or impossible to demonstrate:

> How do you measure quality? Where it's compulsory for students to attend, measures of quality get blurred. It's different in unemployment courses, where students can vote with their feet. (Educational Consultant)

It can't. You can never prove innocence. There are no facts, only local perceptions. (CGLI Officer)

Some respondents advocated the 'demonstration' of proof in the form of advertising and image building:

We are full of hype. The first 30 feet of a store is clear, but back stage . . . (Personnel Manager, large food chain)

Publicity and public relations: my local college has been advertising an open week for small businesses. (BTEC Officer)

CFEs can use local radio to advertise via 'phone-ins'. (Conservative MP)

Colleges have to maintain their image. Shire counties with one college per town have a high profile. The city college is more anonymous. (Assistant Education Officer, large industrial connurbation)

The college needs to do a better job of marketing itself. I'm not sure it can prove anything, but it needs better communication. **Responsibility and responsiveness** is a good example of how it can be done. (FEU Officer)

One principal had undertaken a personal advertising campaign:

I wrote to Sir Keith after **Training for jobs.** I got each head to write. We sent job placement figures[1] and adult retraining statistics. Also the numbers of staff going out to industry . . . We sent him the annual report. He said we were the exception that proved the rule.

A Director of Education saw the institutional data as a source of verification:

Lecturers' backgrounds, time spent linking with industry, lecturers' knowledge of industry . . . some lecturers being from industry . . . attendance with industry on liaison committees. Colleges could claim all this in their defence, and it should not be taken lightly.

and another principal argued similarly for college history:

Go through recent history and college examples. Show how the college has done what it said it would have wanted it to do.

Sixteen respondents volunteered responsiveness indicators, some of

1. Although in interview he admitted that the college did not follow up student leavers very successfully.

them additional to the previous list of criteria: liaison/consultation with employers/local population: market research: a flexible and varied programme of activities; in-service training arrangements; innovative work; effective guidance and counselling provision; satisfaction of employers and students (including the unemployed); employer support, as reflected in unsolicited telephone conversations with local firms' training managers; anecdotal evidence; attitudinal surveys; a consistent view of the labour market; the ability to meet target figures; and speed of response:

> Responsiveness is in the eye of the beholder. But you can measure lead time, the reaction to disaster. That's why industry likes the X Consortium. It's a one-stop shop. There's one place to complain to. (Educational Consultant)

Six of this group saw change as in itself evidence of responsiveness: new markets, new courses, new course content, new delivery modes, timetable changes occasioned by client need rather than institutional convenience, and, from an HMI, 'the amount of change over time'.

Two respondents were approving of HMI methods:

> It's difficult to prove. You can't score colleges. Each college has a different context. There are economic circumstances in the locality. You have to take a case study, like the HMI do. (Director of Education)

> Achievement has to be measured. HMI approaches are OK. (Labour MP)

An LEA Senior Adviser saw self-evaluation as the appropriate response:

> CFEs should be evaluating what they are doing, not leave it only to HMI and advisers.

An industrial training adviser saw real proof as obtainable only by personal investigation:

> I am a poacher turned gamekeeper. I've taught the courses. We have a legal requirement to visit CFEs . . . so I can tell if they are lying or not.

A LA Central Training Officer doubted the results of external moderation:

> We can compare colleges, compare BTEC graduates, but it is not scientific. It's a question of impressions. It is difficult to know about standards of qualifications. The BTEC moderator may reinforce the CFE's courses . . . he/she could be a crucial figure, but they do their jobs differently. In BTEC everyone passes who finishes, but there are no clear grades, so standards are blurred.

A validating body respondent saw the record of examination entry as itself a demonstration of responsiveness:

> The main criteria for responsiveness is whether something is used. People always will complain. You get stresses and strains. Seventy per cent of what we do is demanded by only thirty per cent. Look at the records of candidate entry: there are 1021 examinations. Is that responsiveness enough? Of the 1021, 180 provide for 85 per cent of candidates. There are 2200 exam centres, and 80 per cent of candidates come from 18 per cent of the centres. I would argue that colleges are responsive.

A Labour MP had doubts about both measuring and what one might measure:

> Given MSC's record, they will set up crude control based on finance and won't serve students' or employers' needs and will make the CFEs worse rather than better. Financial inducements help MSC to get their way. I do not believe staff actually achieve it.

A Conservative MP saw job take-up as an appropriate indicator:

> MSC should ask students if they think the courses will lead to jobs.

as did a college head of department:

> On the question of measuring output, I don't know how you do it. With TOPS courses we measured employment rate: if above 40 per cent, OK. The question is how to find out if students have got a job. Many of mine are sponsored, so I measure examination success.

The issue of whether to concern oneself with inputs or with outputs/outcomes, or both, aroused varied comment:

> We should look at inputs rather than outcomes. MSC will be looking for outcomes . . . You have to decide if you are looking at students or the economic community, e.g. are the students the kind that employers want? If not, it may be the employers' fault. (Educational Consultant)

> We are concerned at the intensity with which inputs are being looked at. We would like to look at outputs of the system: quality, relevance of provision, and how it has been maintained in recent years. (TUC)

> I would produce a file showing a list of requests received by the CFE. I would want to show a dialogue with senior people in industry and MSC and the response (outcome). (Industrial Trainer)

Outcomes in the form of client satisfaction (or otherwise) were advocated by some respondents as an appropriate test of responsiveness:

> ... go to the customers and ask them, but not about the quality of the output. (Industrial Trainer)

> Happy customers: ask them. (Employers Federation Officer)

Another argued for fairly extensive client feedback:

> You can't put too much effort into feedback, particularly with a new course. I would want to find out whether it was well targeted. You can go to students before they leave, and go to employers selectively: it's not difficult if the college has good links. (DES Official)

Some respondents saw such information as most appropriately arriving through informal channels:

> We get feedback from industry about the quality of our graduates, on both performance and verbal communication. We had to do some work on the latter to improve it. (Head of Department)

> Encourage moderators to talk to students. They're honest. Follow up the leads. (BTEC Regional Coordinator)

However, a LA Central Training Officer claimed to do precisely this, with no discernible improvement:

> We know that some lecturers are not good enough, and we have made representations, but they are still there. Some lecturers are not interested. They turn up late. We know because we listen to our students, but the head of department tells us that he/she knows the staff. But we are paying (under YTS) for this tuition. It's a question of professional practice.

Some respondents saw questionnaires as an appropriate research instrument:

> There should be systematic questionnaires of students and customers. You hand over your child to the state for eleven years and no one questions you, but on a three-week YTS course, one and one-half weeks are spent on questionnaires. We should be questioning customers: students, parents, local industry[2]. The older the student is, the more relevant his views are. (DES Official)

2. As also suggested by the head of department above, MSC staff devote considerable energy to exploring client reactions and in attempting to follow up leavers. A Manpower Memo (May, 1985) suggests that (based on a postal questionnaire sent to a 15 per cent sample), of the previous summer's YTS leavers, 60 per cent went into employment and 10 per cent into FE or training. Follow-up work is discussed in the next chapter.

I'm in favour of questionnaires and staff appraisal. Our senior staff attend appraisal training sessions. Some employers are wary, but it needs to be put in a positive way. (ITB Officer)

After the announcement of the NAFE 'clawback', principals should have done a questionnaire of local employers to refute non-responsiveness, and lobbied MSC area office. (SDP Spokesperson)

Another group of respondents saw questionnaires as of doubtful value:

I'm hesitant about a blanket answer to formal appraisal. Most CFEs don't use it enough. I wouldn't want to see every college jumping in. What will they do with the damned information once they've got it? There is room for formal appraisal techniques, but if there's only one way of keeping a line on how the college is responding to customers, we could miss something important. Staff would need help: how to distribute and analyse questionnaires. The average lecturer concentrates on formal input: numbers. (MSC Officer)

I'm not particularly interested in questionnaires or performance appraisal. I prefer some form of independent review of customers. The customers are immature. (MSC Officer)

If the system works, would you need to question employers? I am wary of questionnaires. What do you do with the information? I believe in performance appraisal, but it's not easy to say how to do it. (ITB Officer)

Of course, questionnaires are likely to reveal dissatisfaction not only with the college, but with the employer or sponsor, and this concern seems to have been hinted at by another ITB respondent:

Questionnaires are useful and dangerous. If the college is mainly providing courses on prescription, it's dangerous to start questioning the course. I wouldn't ask students. With a college which is the sponsoring body and is offering examinable and non-examinable courses, they should be asking if students understand and if the work is clearly presented and in the right order. I feel they do this well at present. They will get into difficulty if they start questioning the courses of paying customers.

One respondent seemed to have doubts about the value of *any* feedback evidence:

Employers find it hard to formulate their views. They can't know what influences have contributed to the person's confidence.

> How do you ask a small garage proprietor to tell . . . In ten or twenty years students might realise the value of what they're doing, but they can't assess it at this moment in time. There's an act of faith involved in responsiveness. (DES Official)

Among our respondents, by far the most elaborate attempts to analyse delivery described to us was that undertaken by the manufacturing firm which mounted training packages for purchasers of its equipment:

> I get feedback. Did we effect training at the right time and to the standard agreed? Was the training that we gave appropriate training? Could trainees take over the plant? We make video recordings of the training sessions of the chaps we provide and then analyse the video. By and large these have been satisfactory, but we have made some improvements.

Given many of the attitudes revealed in the above quotations, it is hardly unexpected that the MSC/LAA (1985) **Report** should conclude, after a study of 45 colleges in eight LEA areas and one response from a CELP LEA with three colleges, that

> Evaluation of follow-up information was collected spasmodically. Some colleges had a set policy to follow-up courses on a selective basis.

I would suggest that an effective quality control system needs to be formal i.e. regular, systematic and organised, a normal part of operational activity. An informal system is, by definition, occasional, haphazard and accidental, relying, with reference to some of our respondent suggestions, on unsolicited telephone conversations and anecdotal evidence. The purpose of a quality control system is to ensure that delivery and performance are effective, so that outcomes are as closely matched as possible to objectives. Resistance to any kind of quality control procedures appears to be deeply embedded among teacher professionals, so it is perhaps useful to rehearse the major approaches available, and their advantages/disadvantages. The focus is on the kinds of evidence to be collected, and the significant dimensions centre on when, how and by whom.

1. The gathering of evidence can be either **formative/continual** or **summative/terminal,** i.e. it can focus on the activity while it is in operation, frequently with a view to modifying its subsequent progress, or it can be undertaken at the activity's conclusion. Formative evidence is generally most useful with new courses/programmes, since it charts developments and assists with the location of unexpected snags, leaving the provider with the option of altering subsequent delivery. On the other hand, it is generally time consuming (and hence expensive) and can sometimes seem tiresome, somewhat like analysing each bite of a meal. Summative data allows the whole experience to be viewed as a totality, so that what might initially

appear pointless can eventually be seen to be useful, but it provides no opportunity to right unforeseen wrongs. Of course, both formative and summative evidence can be collected, and sometimes are.

2. The major kinds of evidence available to college collection are:

a) **Recorded behaviour:** attendance patterns and drop-out rates give possible leads to client dissatisfaction, but they can also be explained in terms of other variables, e.g. more seductive attractions (exceptional good weather, a sporting fixture), or sudden departure to full-time employment. The Audit Commission (1985) has (perhaps understandably) tended to emphasise the more serious possibilities:

> Low retention rates represent a waste of resources and a loss of opportunity for students who might have completed courses had they been able to secure a place. These losses could be rooted in a number of factors including poor marketing, poor course control, inappropriate curriculum, inadequate teaching, poor student selection and financial hardship. While poor retention rates in themselves are not absolute measures of performance, they certainly indicate where enquiry is merited.

b) Another kind of evidence is **observed behaviour,** which can be perceived either in the classroom/workshop or in the workplace.

c) **Client testimony** can be either **solicited** or **unsolicited.** The latter variety may arrive in the form of complaints or thanks via letters/telephone calls/personal appearances. It is frequently difficult to know whether the information conveyed is representative or exceptional. It is also impossible to conclude that the appearance of no unsolicited testimony is a cause for rejoicing or anxiety. On the other hand, solicited client testimony allows for the possibility of obtaining a representative sample[3] and is usually collected in the form of:

i) **Questionnaires/forms.** These are inevitably impersonal and, unless one stands over the respondents, may result in very low returns. Questionnaires-/forms also have a tendency to impose a 'shape' on client responses, and may upon occasion even 'lead' the recipients, but they have the virtues of being relatively inexpensive, ideally providing a large volume of easily quantifiable data.

ii) **Interviews/discussions** can be conducted on one-to-one, small group or

3. In an FEU commissioned feasibility study of the extent to which an external marketing researcher could advise and support FE colleges in their marketing, HR & H Marketing Research (1985) recommend: 'Systematic surveying of past and present students is of vital importance. Due to the relatively small number of students who would be polled about a particular course, surveys are likely to be of a size manageable by the college. Research consultants could play an important part by providing a questionnaire design consultancy and advising on computer analysis'.

whole group bases. The smaller the group and the larger the number of interviews/discussions, the greater the cost. This approach allows the respondents more opportunities to structure the experience to their own ends and can offer the potentiality for a deeper and fuller expression of individual attitudes, but the resulting data is often so diverse as to render tidy quantification difficult, as this present exercise will have made abundantly clear.

d) **Output and outcomes.** Under this heading we would have to include, where appropriate, student work, examination results, and employment take-up. Once again, there are many variables which may have influenced results: examination failure/pass may be attributed to student/teacher performance; unemployment may be occasioned by forces beyond the influence of either the student or the college. On the other hand, the Audit Commission (1985) argues that

> Few colleges follow the MSC practice of asking former students whether they are in employment, whether that employment makes use of taught skills and what they thought of the courses.

3. In our education/training system, actual evidence tends to be taken by[4]:

a) **External examiners/moderators,** who by their externality can potentially offer a useful basis for comparison across the system, but who cannot necessarily know the particular college situation very fully, since they tend to appear at the output/outcome stage.

b) **The inspectorate (HMIs, LA inspectors/advisers).** As with a) above, they provide the possibility for neutral assessment, but they are notoriously few in number, and their appearances (at least from an institutional point of view) tend to be sporadic and unpredictable.

c) **College senior management,** who are theoretically empowered to institute quality control mechanisms but (so far as FESC evidence can be relied upon) seldom do so on a regular basis for a variety of plausible and non-plausible reasons.

d) **Peers.** In team-teaching situations, one's equals (and sometimes even one's superordinates) are likely to gather evidence about the teaching-/learning activity. Those similarly engaged are likely to have a clearer grasp of the difficulties and hence possess the advantage (or disadvantage) of a sympathetic predisposition[5].

4. If the collector of evidence is not a disinterested individual and/or the respondent cannot remain anonymous, it is difficult to allay the suspicion that the evidence may not be complete or may not represent the respondent's true feelings. Hence, I have here omitted the possibility of the teacher questioning students about his/her own delivery.
5. On the other hand, if they are in competition/envious/less effective in performance, their sympathy may be called into doubt.

e) **Course committees.** In Britain, these are frequently an HE device, with membership drawn from representatives of interested groups: students, college management, teachers, and, when appropriate, the validating body. In NAFE they may also involve employer representation. Committee members serve as 'channels' for evidence directed by their constituents towards other committee members.

f) **Video.** It is sometimes claimed that the presence of a camera intimidates performers and consequently falsifies the performance, against which must be set the possibility of viewing and reviewing by everyone and anyone, including those recorded.

g) **Self-evaluation.** This is a device much recommended by the FEU and possessed of obvious attractions from an individual point of view. However, while it is often considered agreeable among teachers if it involves other teachers, among all such teachers it is less acceptable when it is practised by solicitors, bank managers and politicians.

What the above listing ought to make abundantly clear is that a large number of quality control mechanisms, and a considerable amount of related experience, are already to be found within the system. However, from the perspective of a client, little of it is formal, i.e. regular, systematic and organised. Moreover, whatever the purposes to which the data is actually put, very little appears to be available to defend the system against the charges of detractors. Thus, confronted by the trumpet blast of **Training for jobs,** the system can do little more than answer with an operatic off-stage fanfare in the shape of **Responsibility and responsiveness:** blast and counter-blast, assertion and counter-assertion.

Nor is it only the colleges which appear to lack such data, for their employers, the LEAs, seem equally bereft of evidence. Of course, at an informal level, evidence exists in the shape of anecdote and unsubstantiated conclusion, but the dilemma with informal evidence is that it has to be offered off the record and *sotto voce.* At the same time, formally collected evidence would appear to be essential if any kind of rational staff development policy is to be evolved: without reference to staff and course programme delivery, how can needs be identified? If colleges are to go to employers to identify their needs, rather than relying on what happens to surface at advisory committee meetings, why are similar enquiry methods not to be employed in the college workplace to identify staff development needs?

The importance of staff development was stressed by many of our respondents e.g.

> We need to treat training and education as an investment rather than a cost. In Germany they invest in the country. Here people are afraid they will lose staff. (ITB Officer)

Colleges avoid the staff development role. We need to promote the use of remission for staff development, both formally and informally. (MSC Officer)

Yet it was fairly obvious that staff development represents a custom more 'honour'd in the breach than the observance':

Secondment of FE teachers is very important, but staff get blocked somewhere. Secondment is not seen as in-service training as it doesn't lead to qualifications, but a responsive college would have staff looking for secondment. (Chamber of Commerce Officer)

I'd like to see lecturers go back into industry to update themselves. Technology changes, but the attitude of the workforce also changes. Ten years ago you could say to a team, 'Do a job', but today the team is better educated, more highly paid, and has a greater ability to reason, so they ask questions and demand more of college lecturers. (Industrial Trainer)

Lecturers should update themselves on applications, i.e. what you can do with new technology, and they must be happy to admit that they are ignorant. They should see themselves as 'access men' to relevant learning, which may not necessarily be in the college. (Employers Federation Officer)

Many of these points are substantiated by the MSC/LAA (1985) **Report** which concludes that many teachers

... are not equipped ... to meet their own needs to keep abreast of developments in industry, commerce and new technology.

and stresses, from its study of eight LEAs, that

The amount of finance and time available for staff development was not always felt to be adequate.

a deficiency noted by the Audit Commission (1985) in its suggestion that, 'Academic staff development ... needs to be allowed for', having blamed the lack of provision on inefficient deployment of staffing resources.

However, the current scarcity of available time for staff development activities does not appear to have led to a more careful scrutiny of how such time might be most profitably used. In the first place, without throughput monitoring and output analysis, it becomes difficult to establish precisely who needs staff development and of what particular kind:

You can't have staff development provision without appraisal. Many colleges and departments are deficient in appraisal approaches, which is why staff development is deficient. There

are many examples of effective appraisal, but I do not like the civil service approach with ticks on paper. There are a variety of ways we could use. The staff development role needs to be accepted ...
(MSC Officer)

Secondly, monitoring is also required of the benefits/limitations of different kinds of in-service industrial experience, i.e. whether, as one of our respondent principals claimed, nothing less than a full year could be meaningful, or whether a variety of attendance patterns could be profitably employed, and the deficiencies for which each kind is most appropriate. Without agreed performance indicators, staff development needs not only remain difficult to identify, but prescription is difficult to substantiate. The sceptic in search of a sound investment might well wish to know who needs what, why, when, where, how and for how long.

There is neither time nor space at this junction to explore all of the rationalisations which are advanced to justify the present antipathy to identifying performance indicators and output measures, but it will be useful to confront those most frequently offered:

1. **The clients are unfit to pass judgement.** We have already seen it asserted that employers are incapable of articulating their needs and of evaluating course/programme outcomes. To this is frequently added the alleged immaturity of (many) students. There appears to be an underlying conviction that clients are incapable of making a valid final judgement, a conclusion which it would be difficult to refute if one thinks in terms of high court judges, chief examiners and external moderators. By comparison, college clients are largely 'immature', whatever their ages, for they lack the requisite knowledge and experience. However, valid or not, clients do make judgements, just as we all do of one another throughout the most casual and trivial of encounters, as well as upon extended acquaintance. Feedback is not concerned with passing sentence on performers, but with exteriorising and utilising client reactions to as to render delivery more effective. There is something inordinately strange, and difficult to defend, in a major service industry whose professionals positively do not want to know what their clients think and feel.

2. **The real value of education/training is likely to remain invisible for ten or twenty years.** This assertion brings to mind a kind of long-term credit card: with a few decades in which to pay the bills, it is almost impossible to resist impulse buying. With teaching, the bills are unlikely ever to be delivered, since all partners will have moved on long before. However, this allegation is becoming increasingly difficult to sustain. The likelihood is not that the benefits of education/training cannot be appreciated for a score of years, but that long before that the actual experience will have become obsolete, a realisation underlying the CNAA insistence on recent signs of intellectual activity among course proposal staffing resources. The rate of change and

the advancement of knowledge and technology - not least in industry/commerce - present educators/trainers with the problem of keeping up with tomorrow, never mind the remote future.

3. **What is of real value in education/training cannot be measured or, in some instances, even seen.** Here, of course, the missionary comes to the fore, and is irrefutable. Insofar as education is an 'act of faith', an attribute bestowed upon responsiveness by one of our respondents, one cannot devise performance indicators. The transcendental is by definition beyond both reach and sight.

However, the last assertion, even if unanswerable, effectively makes the central point. The debate against quality control devices and the introduction of formal throughput monitoring tends to be conducted on a divide and rule basis. None of the approaches described above can be said to be without limitations: individually each is inadequate. Collectively, a package or group of approaches helps to balance some of the deficiencies of some with the strengths of others, but, even so, it would be difficult to argue that what one is left with is a model of perfection. But then, why should it be? In a persuasively argued case for 'The Evaluation of Training', Morris (1984) sums up succinctly:

> Training evaluation is not an exact science. It is not in the nature of human processes that they should be subject to scientifically and clearly defined rules. The variables are too many. Nonetheless, these potential difficulties must not be seen as excuses for ducking the issue. If as trainers we can identify, set up and measure necessary foundation stones and milestones for our activities then we can reasonably claim reasonable bases for justifying our contribution to the business enterprise.

It seems unlikely that CFEs will willingly embrace throughput monitoring as a consequence of exhortation or argument. What is more likely to effect such a change is an instinct for survival. Criticism evokes defensiveness, which in turn stimulates a search for weapons. Both CFEs and their local authorities have recently come under attack from Government **(Training for jobs)**, NEDC/MSC **(Competence and competition)**, and the Audit Commission, of which the last is potentially the most damaging with its revelations of non-management of resources in many institutions. Moreover, the CFE clientele is likely to continue to change in coming years in the present direction of being more, rather than less, demanding; and competition from private-sector provision, particularly in the more lucrative markets, will have an additionally sobering effect. In such circumstances, performance indicators and output measures may come to be recognised as a hitherto ignored source of ammunition. Agreed criteria for responsiveness, and an ability to prove the existence of responsiveness with hard and soft (even if imperfect) data, could give CFEs (and their LEAs) the kind of evidence they have thus far been unable to muster.

Summary

The absence of formal (regular, systematic and organised) quality control devices, of general college or system agreement about performance indicators and output measures, was reflected in answers respondents gave to questions about the criteria used to identify/measure responsiveness. Forty-seven variables were offered, the majority suggesting a broad commitment among our sample to data collection based on subjective evaluation, intuitive judgement, hunch and 'feel'. Among those (approximately four-fifths of the total) who offered criteria for identifying college responsiveness, less than a fifth suggested that responsiveness ought to be viewed in terms of the whole provision process, input/throughput/output, intention/delivery/outcomes.

A brief survey was provided of data collection processes currently available for gauging responsiveness (the kinds of evidence, when-/how/by whom collected, advantages/disadvantages), but it was suggested that these processes have little general support across the profession, although they offer possible access to client reactions and a potentially useful (if imperfect) means to establishing the relative degree of satisfaction/responsiveness, so that existing provision might be modified/adapted in the direction of improved delivery. It was finally argued that such data would additionally resolve current debate about college/employer responsiveness.

Chapter 9

AFTER-SALES SERVICE: WAS IT WORTH THE MONEY?

The reader who has persevered thus far may have noticed an omission, or at least a focus of infrequent attention: money. Of approximately 350 repondent quotations, fewer than five per cent make direct references to money. There are, to be sure, references to 'socio-economic factors' and the ubiquitous 'resources', but most of the allusions to cash are about whether colleges should be 'profit centres' and who should get the profit. Despite all the discussions about the college as a business, the product cycle and the difficulties of marketing, there is virtually nothing about money from the client/customer's point of view. The emphasis is on effectiveness, rather than efficiency. Only one repondent suggested as a criteria for judging college responsivenenss 'value for money'. One could be forgiven for finding such reticence (or indifference) rather unexpected. As shoppers, most of us look at the price tag at a very early stage in the transaction and tend to view our purchases in terms of cost benefit: was it worth the money?

It is possible that we as interviewers, and the topic of our project, directed our respondents away from a direct consultation of financial issues, but then commercial 'responsiveness' would normally have to encompass provision at a cost which the customer was willing/able to pay. The more likely explanation is that education/training in CFEs has been traditionally financed almost wholly via rates and the Rate Support Grant channelled through the LA treasurer's department, with varied sums arriving by tuition fees. An interesting document recently made available to FESC by an LA Officer (Bower, 1985) argues that tuition fees represent a 'declining proportion of income in an area of high unemployment with a remission policy', and suggests that, despite

> . . . the Local Authority Association's objections to the principle of Specific Grants for education, these are now a reality in all LEAs not only at the margins but increasingly at the mainstream of provision.

There follows a list of more than 30 sources ('not necessarily comprehensive') which includes: MSC, ITBs, PICKUP, OPEN TECH, ALBSU, REPLAN, ERDF, ECSC, Urban Aid, ESF, FEU, ESG, LGTB, MEP, CELP, EOC, etc[1]. Employees are identified as a

1. As well as noting LEA 'discretionary payment', and payments 'from the MSC through YTS allowances and the DHSS for part-time attendance under the 21 hour rule. This list raises many issues about the future of the system . . . the stability of the system when finance is made available increasingly on a pump-priming or short-term contractual basis'. What it does, of course, is to promote a market approach and to shift power (in the form of demand) from the provider to the client.

Declining source of income to support the age group up to 19; but growth possibilities for supporting 'full cost' courses for adults under the Adult Training Strategy.

What we have is a market segmentation process conducted by means of specific grants, with control shifting away from local governments towards central government (and EEC) agencies acting as secondary clients buying in provision on behalf of identified primary client groups[2]. The assumption is that human beings spend their own money more carefully than they do someone else's money. On the evidence provided by the Audit Commission (1985), it is difficult to deny that at least in some CFEs money has been used in a somewhat cavalier fashion:

Non-teaching time in a working week of 30 hours and the two non-teaching weeks in the working year are intended to provide for preparation, marking, administration, enrolment etc. However, it is relatively unusual to find any reliable information on how this time is used. Lack of hard information must be a handicap to good staff utilisation.

Auditors found that remission was given on widely differing bases and that the average in colleges ranged from almost zero to 24 per cent of all contact hours . . . In some colleges most remission is given to senior staff who already have fewest contact hours.

The MSC has observed that essentially the same course taking 18 weeks at one college takes as long as 26 weeks at another; and the colleges involved found it difficult to provide a rationale for the difference.

If, as individuals, we were employing someone to paint our house, dig our garden, or teach us to drive, we might be more concerned to ensure that our money was well spent and that those we employed performed efficiently. One of the consequences of the Specific Grant system currently evolving is that funders tend to scrutinise their own purchases much more systematically and rigorously, as the Audit Commission again makes clear by comparison:

Few colleges follow the MSC practice of asking former students whether they are in employment[3], whether that employment makes use of taught skills and what they thought of the courses. But some colleges do circularise 'drop outs' to find out the reasons for their failure to complete their studies; others, like Worthing, undertake in-depth market research of specific course

2. But also individuals, if we recall the voucher scheme noted earlier.
3. The Danish experience (Theodossin, 1984) indicates that the demands of paying customers are a fundamental stimulus to system monitoring and modification.

requirements; and some follow the practice of Norwich City College of tracking the employment record of their students after graduation.

To the above list we might add the practice of some colleges of soliciting feedback both in the college and the workplace with full-cost short courses mounted for local employers, particularly where there is a possibility of re-running the same course. In new provision, most of the development costs are likely to be absorbed in the introductory phase.

However, the kinds of omissions which we have been exploring - the lack of systematic and regular use of performance indicators, output measures and after-sales servicing[4] - cannot be laid entirely at the proverbial feet of CFEs. The college and the student have a relationship, and all relationships are at least two-sided. If the college has been traditionally somewhat remiss in monitoring the use of public funds, so, we might argue, has the student, and for similar reasons.

Competence and competition provides some interesting contrasts in comparing German, US, Japanese and UK education/training experiences. The 1981 statistics show that larger proportions of those aged 16-24 participate in the three overseas countries. The report also points out that in the US

Post-secondary students are expected to pay for VET unless it is provided free by an employer. The proportion of institutional costs covered by tuition fees varies between the public and private sector. There is extensive provision for loans, grants, scholarships and part-time work.

and concludes that in the UK

The private cost cannot be estimated but (unlike Japan and the US) is only a small proportion.

Some European countries also promote student loan systems, again with a view to reducing public spending, but also to facilitate consumerism in what is essentially market-led provision. Where students are paying directly for what they receive, they are likely to be more demanding[5]. Again, **Competence and competition** makes explicit the kinds of after-sales service US students expect:

The output of vocational programmes in two-year colleges is

4. Corroborated by HR & H Marketing Research (1985): 'Systematic, formal, regular follow-ups of past students are virtually non-existent'.
5. So, too, are employers, if they can be persuaded to contribute a larger proportion to existing training costs and/or to sponsor more extended and extensive training. The MSC, in association with the National Economic Development Office, has commissioned a 'major study to examine ways of encouraging British employers to invest more in vocational education and training' (Press Notice, 22 April 1985)

generally directed towards employment . . . Students are assisted in finding jobs by Job Placement Offices which list openings, arrange interviews with visiting employers and help with job search, resumé writing and interview preparation. Separate college counselling services offer opportunities for self-assessment and career/life planning.

Although proprietary schools charge tuition fees . . . they claim two advantages over community and technical colleges. First they aim to train people as quickly and efficiently as possible. Secondly, they ensure their students get jobs after graduating - some devoting extensive resources to the job placement activity. One school, from which about 850 engineering and computer programming technicians graduate annually, employs 10 people full-time and several part-time lead-chasers in other parts of the country, just to place graduates in employment.

In our interviews (limited, of course, with reference to specific colleges), there was virtually no evidence of any kind of after-sales provision, certainly not in the form of an institutional approach that was systematic, regular and organised. There was some suggestion that some departments were better than others in following up students. Yet, after-sales servicing can be said to provide useful advantages for colleges as well as ex-students:

1. It can serve as a venue for market-research in that access to local firms to follow up student progress in the workplace can be combined with information updating and the identification of new needs/developments.

2. The experience of ex-students putting their training into practice can be used in reviewing the subsequent provision of their courses/programmes and can allow for informed modification.

3. Employer/ex-student satisfaction can form the basis on which to sell additional CFE courses/programmes to ex-customers.

In all of the above ways, the after-sales and the early-cycle marketing activities become intertwined. In systems terms, feedback is used to modify input and throughput. The product cycle spirals back so that each sequence of the process informs, and is informed by, other sequences:

It is difficult to see how colleges can understand how well individual courses are meeting the needs of the market unless they make systematic attempts to obtain specific feedback from the market place. This could take the form of:
- student reports at the end of each session;
- 'exit' interviews with students dropping out: why do individuals not continue on courses for which they have enrolled?

- follow-up with students who have completed courses, say six months later; with hindsight (which is always improved) how could the course have met their needs better? (Audit Commission, 1985)

The frequent absence of just such practices can be viewed as something of a refutation of the alleged missionary role in colleges, but it can also be regarded as poor business practice, since it denies staff the possibility of obtaining potentially beneficial and useful information.

Of course, as I have suggested above, the students themselves must be accorded at least some of the blame. It is not merely the absence of any direct and significant financial commitment, but in many cases also their age and the nature of their school experience immediately prior to entering the CFE. However, here, too, we are likely to encounter striking changes in the near future. Not only is there a possibility of more and more secondary clients acting as intermediaries between primary client groups and the college, but the primary clients are themselves due to change:

One important change in the clientele for NAFE is likely to be in increasing participation of adults in training . . . demographic trends show the numbers . . . aged between 16 and 19 declining substantially over the rest of the decade, while the number of those aged 25 to 54 will grow substantially. (MSC/LAA, 1985)

Such a shift in client composition is likely to increase the proportion of those who are prepared to view their college experience more critically and who are likely to make increased demands on college staff.

In marketing terms, CFEs are currently facing a radically changing market-place: many traditional demands are declining; new demands are emerging, accompanied by the need for new skills/techniques/-technologies; the main growth potential lies down market and in the cultivation of full-cost short-course provision; the new market segments are likely to be increasingly challenging in terms of behaviour (uncommitted school leavers) and expectations (adults); competition is growing from a variety of directions: secondary schools fighting to retain their own up-market activities; HE institutions prepared to move down-market into CFE territories; and private industrial trainers seeking to weather an economic recession. In addition, block grant funding is being eroded by the emergence of increasing numbers of entrepreneurial secondary clients in search of the 'best buy' available for the primary clients they represent.

In system terms, organisations survive by responding to environmental demands and by modifying their inputs, throughput and outputs/incomes. The marketing metaphor suggests that CFE control over their destiny lies in confronting and managing the whole of their product cycle: market research, product development, quality control and after-sales service, in taking the lead *in search of excellence* by making explicit and visible the

101

nature and existence of that excellence.

Summary

Our respondents indicated limited interest in college efficiency, as distinct from effectiveness, and provided even less evidence of after-sales servicing, following up student leavers into the workplace (or unemployment), although it should be noted that the nature and limitations of our enquiry may account in part for the omissions. It was argued that the current situation where students are largely funded by the state may make them less demanding clients than some of their overseas counterparts, but that the college scene may well be changing: there is evidence of an increasing tendency towards specific grants for education/training via secondary client representatives, and anticipated changes in the market (shrinking conventional demand, the growth of new client groups) may bring more rigorous and challenging demands to CFEs. Finally, it was suggested that a movement towards after-sales servicing could in itself be seen as a form of market research and data collection which could offer an informed basis for modifying college delivery in the direction of enhanced responsiveness.

Chapter 10

THE RESPONSIVE COLLEGE: SOME CONCLUDING REFLECTIONS

On the basis of our limited research, it would be inappropriate to attempt to draw final conclusions about college responsiveness. What one can suggest is that **Training for jobs** and subsequent central government publications have issued a challenge, thrown down a gauntlet, to which the system has been able to respond only with difficulty and uncertainty. In defence of work-related NAFE, there have been public shows of professional indignation - assertions, denials and rebuttals - behind which one can detect considerable dismay. The allegation that CFEs have failed to meet employer needs has tended to expose the following dilemmas in the world of education/training:

1. There is no clear consensus about what the organisational mission of CFEs is/should be. At the interface between the workplace and the college, the traditional commitments/interests of the marketeer and the missionary confront each other uneasily, and are revealed in a series of dichotomies: training vs education, skills-for-others and self-development, now and forever, the distinction between price and value.

2. For many of our respondents, the above dichotomies were confronted in a mood of considerable ambivalence, so that disagreement among the whole sample was often accompanied at the individual level by an uncomfortable awareness of the values of competing perceptions.

3. Much of the ambivalence centres on the marketing function of CFEs, or at least what critics have suggested ought to be the prevailing operational mode of new-style colleges. Among our respondents, few had thought through the implications of a genuinely businesslike approach to running colleges. How commercial should colleges be? In the college-as-business, what are the fundamental motives of the sellers? How does one square the profitable with minority needs, cost effectiveness with range of offerings, demand with need, the group with the individual, income-generation with social concern? Where does one draw the line? And who draws it?

4. It would be difficult to claim that colleges are uniquely provider-centred amidst a service sector which is conspicuously client-centred. However, the argument that employers are incapable of articulating their needs, and/or unable to assess whether they have been met, does tend to hint at an underlying antagonism towards industry/commerce. Firstly, the assertion carries within itself an implicit assumption that colleges have not been

responsive, thereby leading to attack as a form of defence; and secondly it suggests that the onus for satisfaction lies with the client, which is a strange assumption in a service industry. In the real world, the resolution may lie in provider and client working together to define, monitor, modify and evolve both definition and provision.

5. The defensiveness, and the weak arguments, bring us to the fundamental CFE dilemma, *the absence of a valid data base* for substantiating its own convictions and/or refuting those of others. Like their central/local partners, most colleges appear to concentrate almost exclusively, in systems terms, on inputs rather than on throughput, output/outcome, feedback analysis. The absence of internal college quality control mechanisms and after-sales follow-up thus tends to deprive institutions of valuable information which could help in identifying client needs/reactions and in improving delivery. Such information would also establish beyond doubt a commitment to client satisfaction and enable CFEs to silence their critics. However, if there is to be no basis for judgement beyond private impression, hunch and intuition, one person's conclusion is not necessarily more/less valid than another's, as our respondents' list of 47 criteria for judging college responsiveness suggests.

6. While it might be argued that colleges ought to take the lead in promoting a broad consensus about CFE goals and values, it could also be claimed (as I have suggested) that in service industries, quality (and hence excellence, for which we set out to search) lies in the eye of the beholder, or occasionally in the ear of the persuaded. If that were true, then real responsiveness would be a function of individual/customised provision, in which case monitoring the levels of client satisfaction would be a fundamental management task for the responsive college, and responding more effectively would be demonstrable in terms of raised levels of client satisfaction.

INTERVIEW SCHEDULE

What is the purpose/function of CFEs?

What is a responsive college?/What does the phrase the responsive college mean to you?

To whom should the college be responding: Students, government/HMI, MSC, local authorities, parents, employers, validating/examining bodies/-agencies, professional bodies/ITBs, teachers?

What ought the college do in the event of disagreement/conflict among its clients?
Whom would you put at the top and bottom of the list?

What criteria do you use to decide whether the college is responsive?

How can a college prove its responsiveness?

Which (if any) college(s) do you perceive as particularly responsive?

What distinguishes this (these) organisation(s): individuals, structure(s), situation/setting?

If you had central (or local) power over a group of colleges, what change(s) would you advocate to increase responsiveness?

What do you perceive as the main obstacle(s) to responsiveness?

What characterises the non-responsive college(s)?

To what extent would you support commercial activities in CFEs?

Is there anything I haven't asked which you think I should have, or anything else you would like to say?

THE PRODUCT CYCLE: A SYSTEMS VIEW OF THE MARKETING PROCESS

An open system model can be adapted to represent the activity of a single college, as in Figure 1:

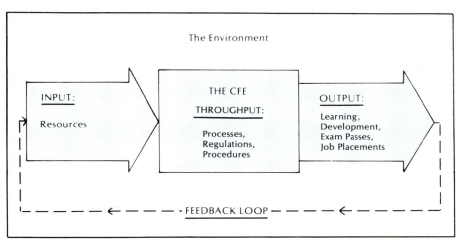

Figure 1: CFE activity depicted as an open system.

1. The environment provides the system with **INPUT** in the form of resources, i.e. anything which is useful and/or necessary to get the job done. In the case of a CFE, INPUT would have to be thought of as including staff (their skills, knowledge, commitment), students (their prior learning, abilities, commitment), curriculum/syllabi, funds, books and materials, equipment, buildings, heating and lighting, etc.

2. **THROUGHPUT** is the term used to describe what happens to the INPUT in the system, the processes, regulations and procedures through which the INPUT passes, here depicted as the CFE and sometimes described as a 'black box' because what happens in the system is largely invisible from the environment, like the contents of a black box.

3. The system produces **OUTPUT** - or, some educationists would claim, **OUTCOMES** - which in the case of a college can be thought of as learning,

qualifications, personal relationships, individual development, job placements and so on.

4. However, OUTPUT does not pass into the environment without effect. One of the OUTCOMES of both the THROUGHPUT and the OUTPUT can be expressed in terms of client satisfaction, in the case of work-related NAFE encompassing both college-leavers and employers who receive them. High levels of client satisfaction may lead to increased demand and an enhanced reputation for the CFE; low client satisfaction levels may result in complaints, reduced demand and/or a search for alternative provision. The consequence(s) of OUTPUT, and the ways in which those consequences impact on the environment and possibly on subsequent INPUT, is called **FEEDBACK.**

As noted above, the systems perspective is essentially a metaphor designed to conceptualise the overall activity process of (in this case) the CFE, as well as the component mechanisms of that process. Of course, like all metaphors, the conceptualisation is a simplification, but that in itself is potentially useful for highlighting crucial areas of activity. The emphasis in the systems view is on the relationship between the organisation and the community (environment) of which it is a part. The underlying assumptions are that the CFE and the community affect each other, but that the relationship is unbalanced, with the college much more influenced by the community than the latter is by the former. There are further assumptions as well: that

1. While INPUT is significantly a function of environmental constraints, demands and influences, not least in terms of what kinds of client groups are actually available, there is still a possibility of the CFE exercising **some control,** e.g. by filtering/guiding/counselling/accepting/rejecting potential students and through staff selection/retraining, income-generating activities, curriculum innovation/modification, etc. A new principal will almost certainly find that his/her ability to affect inputs is severely limited, but not totally so, and over time the principal may effect significant changes. Of course, both individual ability and the environmental estate (benign/turbulent) will affect the possibilities.

2. Although constrained by a host of legal/cultural restrictions (conditions of service, professional behaviour norms), THROUGHPUT is an area over which staff have **more control.** Here it is that managers manage, or fail to do so. It is at this point that inventive principals 'bend' the regulations and oversee (depending on their success) effective/ineffective delivery.

3. OUTPUT is an area over which the CFE has **virtually no control,** although it may influence, for example, examination passes where there is either some continual and/or internal assessment. However, OUTPUT is the end of the process, the consequence of what has come before. So, too, are OUTCOMES and FEEDBACK, and at this point the college can do little more

than scrutinise (e.g. examination results) and analyse in an attempt to glean information which might serve as a subsequent input and be used to modify later throughput.

In order to provide a framework for analysing the rest of our research data, it will be useful to seek to integrate the notion of a product cycle into the above systems conceptualisation. The product cycle model represents very much of an ideal state view, what might be expected to happen in a perfect world, where the CFE lecturer as a marketeer might be urged to undertake the following activities:

1. **Market research.** On the assumption that what the CFE offers is an organised/structured learning experience over time, and to assist in the manufacture of education/training courses/programmes, our hypothetical lecturer should begin with market research. He should seek to identify existing/potential client groups and to ascertain what they need/want. This information represents part of the input and ought to be employed in the next stage.

2. **Product development, selling and promoting.** On the basis of what he has gleaned from his market research, the lecturer/marketeer should organise the production of appropriate and relevant courses, programmes of study, training and other services intended to satisfy identified needs/wants. This activity may require negotiation both within (among colleagues) and outside (with validating bodies, the LEA) the institution. The new product will ultimately represent an input into the system. The lecturer's task will now be to inform the waiting world of the possibilities suddenly available. As a good entrepreneur, he will be attempting to influence output, principally by generating demand.

At this point we might pause to observe that the marketeer will thus far have been reactive in seeking to find out what others need/want and in responding to what has been identified, but proactive in going to them, in creating what he hopes conforms to their expectations and in taking the good news to them. He might have been more proactive (but primarily unresponsive) in manufacturing his new courses/programmes, or repackaging the old ones, and then seeking to sell what he has to individuals who may or may not benefit from the exchange. In either case, he will have been concerned with promoting both his own interest and that of others, although which he chooses to emphasise, or privately considers the more important, may vary from time to time. In any event, all of the above activities will have been concerned with identifying/encouraging/-influencing input. Theoretically he may end up with no takers, either because his research failed or because the needs/wants he identified changed significantly between his locating them and being in a position to satisfy them. Therefore all of this activity could eventually prove abortive. Even well researched, carefully designed and ingeniously sold products do not necessarily attract (enough) buyers.

3. **Quality control.** Having attracted sufficient students to run his new course, our marketeer would now turn his attention to the throughput part of the process. He would assume that between the conceptualisation and the realisation all would not necessarily go well. When the plans are translated into the assembly line process, manufacturing inevitably involves unforeseen problems. Therefore, our marketeer would want to establish monitoring techniques for identifying trouble spots along the delivery route. He would look at pacing, sequencing, organisation. He would want to scrutinise the quality of inputs/staff: are they performing effectively, or do they require modification (staff development)? Since he was concerned with people, he would certainly want to examine retention/dropout rates with a view to identifying both what kept some with, and drove others from, the course. He would therefore want *formative evaluation,* periodic spot checks of how things were going, but he would also seek *summative evaluation,* reactions at the conclusion of the course/programme. In systems terms, he would be seeking both an overview, and a detailed knowledge, of the throughput process, with a view to modifying and improving subsequent throughputs. At some future date, when the course/programme had been in operation long enough to establish its ability to achieve client satisfaction, he might reduce the intensity of his scrutiny and opt for routine operational monitoring procedures.

4. **After-sales service.** Once the students had completed their learning experience, our marketeer would want to spend some time analysing both the output/outcomes and the feedback. For the former he would certainly want to reflect (where appropriate) upon the examination results, with a view to identifying satisfactory pass rates, and where they were unacceptable to re-examining the throughput activity. He would also want to follow at least a sample of his ex-students (again where appropriate) into the workplace (or unemployment). This would help him with charting the practical consequences of the course/programme and would, at the same time, constitute fundamental market research. In the workplace, he would want to investigate the reactions/attitudes of both ex-students and their supervisors/employers. At the same time, follow-up activity would provide opportunities for identifying as yet undiscerned needs/wants, for developing new provision, and for selling the existing product range.

5. **Decline and demise.** Eventually all products either satisfy existing (and stimulated) market demand and/or the market itself changes. Our marketeer would have to consider at what point the product needed to be phased out and a new and potentially different alternative be made available.

The whole sequence, from 1 to 5 above, can therefore be seen as a *continual spiralling process* in which 3, 4, and 5 generate information which can be fed back into 1, establishing regular product review/modification/-

replacement in the light of changing employer/employee/individual needs. The process, 1 to 4, is illustrated in Figure 2. Our marketeer would thus be keeping a firm grip on both the market and the college, and the interaction between the two.

Of course some teachers might well challenge the product cycle on the grounds that education is not a manufacturing industry, but, rather, a service industry. The missionary might well want to argue that the course/programme was essentially a vehicle for carrying the message to the unconverted. In at least England and Wales, however, such an assertion would be difficult to substantiate. A cursory glance at most CFE prospectuses would establish indisputably that colleges 'sell' courses, and that courses frequently entail successful prior learning. In Scotland, on the other hand, the recent introduction of a modular Action Plan means that instead of providing courses, colleges will make available a variety of component units which can be assembled within established guidelines to meet individual needs, with the possibility of interrupted education/training and of carrying forward successfully completed modules wholly or partly towards altered curricular destinations. The Action Plan represents a form of *partial customisation* similar to provision available in many North American institutions, a self-assembly system with inherent credit transfer. It also means that there exists a possibility of modifying single modular components of larger programmes without the necessity of altering the whole programme. Negotiated, or contract, learning may be said to make possible, at least theoretically, a form of *total customisation,* since the individual is required to agree a programme with an institutional representative. Market research becomes far less crucial since, with the partial variety, modular selection provides a data base, and with negotiated learning the negotiation is itself a form of market research: both kinds of customisation offer the potential for non- (or nearly non-) identical products. With both there is also a necessity for careful counselling, where effectiveness is dependent on after-sales service, so that a knowledge of the outcomes for last year's leavers can be used to inform the choices of this year's entrants.

We come, inevitably, to the familiar notion of horses for courses. If courses are the 'product', then there is a necessity of ensuring that they are organised to meet the needs of likely horses. On the other hand, if we are into courses for horses, it might be argued that we have moved from a manufacturing to a service industry. In that case, there is no product cycle, rather a servicing sequence, with the emphasis on the client/customer rather than the market stall. In the movement from 1 to 5 above, 1 (market research) diminishes in importance; and 2 (product development, selling and promotion) and 5 (decline and demise) disappear, since no product exists. Moreover, selling and promotion are significantly altered, since what is being sold is not a product but a facility[1]. In service industries, there is

1. Davies and Scribbins (1985) interestingly use only a manufacturing industry analogy in **Marketing further and higher education - a handbook.**

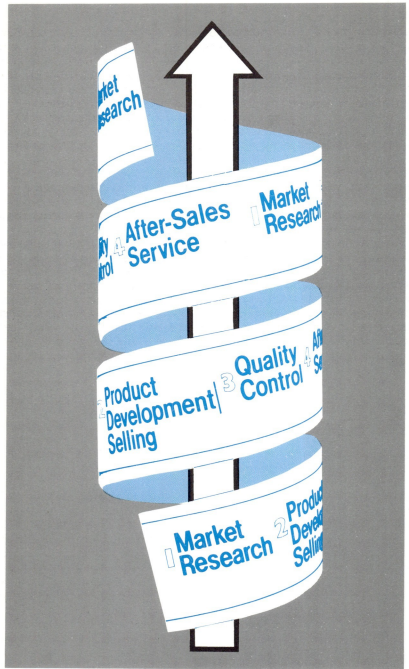

Figure 2: Product cycle spiral.

correspondingly less investment and risk in new product development; modification and adaptation are easier on an incremental basis since provision is not uniform; evolution is less painful than synoptic alteration. At the same time, the emphasis shifts from input to throughput. Who comes is less important than what is done to/with/for them. The role of validating bodies diminishes (or even disappears) since such organisations exist to legitimise products: in a (even partially) customised world, standardisation is impossible, and the validator's last refuge lies in comparability, which in turn becomes progressively difficult as the variations proliferate. Thus, after-sales-service - following the individual to the point where the intention is realised - becomes increasingly crucial.

The systems model holds for either kind of industry, manufacturing or service, or even a hybrid. However, as the nature of the industry is altered, as its focus shifts from finding buyers for products to devising experiences for buyers, the relative importance of the systems components is modified. As we have seen previously, there is again a certain confusion, a half-glimpsed ambivalence, in the current **Competence and competition** exhortation to 'make customers welcome on their own terms', which implies individualisation, unless, of course, the customers happen to come in convenient groups of 30+ (to satisfy the Audit Commission) all with identical needs/wants. A genuine shift to customisation necessitates more than changed attitudes and frequent lecturer journeys to the workplace: it demands significant changes in the way colleges have traditionally worked.

ACRONYMS AND INITIALISMS

Acronyms and initialisms represent part of the professional code through which educationalists/trainers communicate. For the uninitiated, or the forgetful, we offer the following, with apologies for what is (to some) obvious.

ACSET	**Advisory Committee on the Supply and Education of Teachers**
AE	**Adult Education**
AFE	**Advanced Further Education**
AEO	**Assistant Education Officer**
ALBSU	**Adult Literacy and Basic Skills Unit**
APC	**Association of Principals of Colleges**
BTEC	**Business and Technician Education Council**
CBI	**Confederation of British Industry**
CELP	**College Employer Links Project**
CERI	**Centre for Educational Research and Innovation**
CFE	**College of Further Education**
CGLI	**City and Guilds of London Institute**
CNAA	**Council for National Academic Awards**
CSE	**Certificate of Secondary Education**
DE	**Department of Employment**
DES	**Department of Education and Science**
DHSS	**Department of Health and Social Security**
ECSC	**European Coal and Steel Community**
EEC	**European Economic Community**
EOC	**Equal Opportunities Commission**
ERDF	**European Regional Department Fund**
ESF	**European Social Fund**
ESG	**Education Support Grant**
FE	**Further Education**
FESC	**Further Education Staff College**
FEU	**Further Education Unit**
FT	**Full Time**
HMI	**Her Majesty's Inspectorate**
ITB	**Industry Training Board**
LA	**Local Authority**
LAA	**Local Authority Associations**
LCP	**Local Collaborative Project**

LGTB	**Local Government Training Board**
LEA	**Local Education Authority**
MEP	**Microelectronics Education Programme**
MP	**Member of Parliament**
MSC	**Manpower Services Commision**
NAB	**National Advisory Body**
NAFE	**Non-Advanced Further Education**
NATFHE	**National Association of Teachers in Further and Higher Education**
NEDC	**National Economic Development Council**
O/A Levels	**Ordinary and Advanced Levels of The General Certificate of Education**
OECD	**Organisation for Economic Co-operation and Development**
OED	**Oxford English Dictionary**
ONC	**Ordinary National Certificate**
PICKUP	**Professional, Industrial and Commercial Updating**
PT	**Part Time**
RAC	**Regional Advisory Council**
REPLAN	**A DES scheme to promote the development of educational opportunities for unemployed adults**
RSA	**Royal Society of Arts**
RSG	**Rate Support Grant**
SATRO	**Science and Technology Regional Organisation**
TOPS	**Training Opportunities Scheme**
TVEI	**Technical and Vocational Education Initiative**
TUC	**Trades Union Congress**
VET	**Vocational Education and Training**
YOP	**Youth Opportunities Programme**
YTS	**Youth Training Scheme**

REFERENCES

Audit Commission (1985) **Obtaining better value from further education.** ISBN: 0-11-701284-X. HMSO.

Bower, Harry (1985) **Sources of funding education 14-19.** Unpublished.

Bradshaw, David (1984) What's wrong with 'Training for jobs'. **Education.** 22 June.

Burgess, Tyrell & Tom Hinds (1983) Solving the mismatch between responsibility and control. **Education.** 26 August.

Cracknell, David (1983) The richness and diversity of enterprise. **Education.** 11 November.

Davies, Peter & Keith Scribbins (1985) **Marketing FE.** ISBN: 0-582-173515. FEU/Longman.

Department of Education & Science (1982) **Teacher training and preparation for working life.** DES.

Department of Education & Science (1983) **Careers education and guidance in further education.** DES.

Department of Education & Science (1984a) **Education for employees.** DES.

Department of Education & Science (1984b) **College employer links project: a note by DES of development and progress.** DES.

Department of Education and Science (1985a) **Technician Education Council Part-time Higher Certificate Programmes in Engineering.** DES.

Department of Education & Science (1985b) **College employer links project: colleges and employers working together for the benefit of all.** ISBN: 0-85522-160-7. DES.

Department of Employment/Department of Education and Science (1984) **Training for jobs** (Cmnd. 9135) HMSO ISBN: 0-10-191350-8.

Flower, F.D. (1981) **Transition and access.** FEU. ISBN: 0-85522-088-0.

HR & H Marketing Research (1985) **Marketing FE: a feasibility study.** FEU. ISBN: 0-946469-09-1.

Humphrey, Colin & Hywel Thomas (1983a) Making efficient use of scarce resources. **Education.** 12 August.

Humphrey, Colin & Hywel Thomas (1983b) Counting the cost of an experimental scheme. **Education.** 19 August.

Kedney, Bob & David Parkes (eds) (1985) **Responsibility and responsiveness, case studies in further education.** AMA/FESC, Blagdon, Further Education Staff College. ISBN: 0-90769-31-4.

Knight, Brian (1983) Big bang or slow creep? **Education.** 9 December.

Manpower Services Commission/Department of Education & Science (1985) **Review of vocational qualifications in England and Wales: interim report.** MSC. ISBN: 0-86392-127-2.

Manpower Services Commission (1985) **NAFE implementation group discussion paper: the NAFE planning cycle.** MSC.

Manpower Services Commission/Local Authority Associations Policy Group (1985a) **Work-related NAFE: a guidance handbook.** MSC.

Manpower Services Commission/Local Authority Associations (1985b) **MSC/LAA Group on work-related non-advanced further education: report of policy group.** Chairman: Sir Roy Harding. (Unpublished)

Morgan, Colin *et al* (1983) **The selection of secondary school headteachers.** Milton Keynes, Open University Press. ISBN: 0-335-10410-X.

Morris, Michael (1984) The evaluation of training. **ICT.** March/April.

National Economic Development Council/Manpower Services Commission (1984) **Competence and competition: training and education in the Federal Republic of Germany, the United States and Japan.** NEDC. ISBN: 7292-0652-1.

Peters, Thomas J. & Robert H. Waterman (1982) **In search of excellence: lessons from American's best-run companies.** New York, Harper & Row. ISBN: 0-06-015042-0.

TACIT (1985) **Commercial and industrial perceptions of colleges of further education** and **Training for industry in colleges of further education.** (Unpublished)

Theodossin, Ernest (1984) Vocational education and training in Denmark. **FESC Comparative papers in further education** No. 13. Blagdon, Further Education Staff College. ISBN: 0-907659-28-4.